Understanding Career Counselling

Understanding Career Counselling

Theory, Research and Practice

Jennifer M Kidd

SAGE Publications

Los Angeles • London • New Delhi • Singapore

First published 2006 twice
Reprinted 2007

 SAGE Publications Ltd
1 Oliver's Yard
55 City Road
London EC1Y 1SP

SAGE Publications Inc.
2455 Teller Road
Thousand Oaks, California 91320

SAGE Publications India Pvt Ltd
B 1/I1 Mohan Cooperative Industrial Area
Mathura Road, New Delhi 110 044
India

SAGE Publications Asia-Pacific Pte Ltd
33 Pekin Street #02-01
Far East Square
Singapore 048763

British Library Cataloguing in Publication data

A catalogue record for this book is available from the
British Library

ISBN 978-1-4129-0338-7
ISBN 978-1-4129-0339-4 (pbk)

Library of Congress Control Number available

Typeset by C&M Digitals (P) Ltd., Chennai, India
Printed on paper from sustainable resources
Printed and bound in Great Britain by TJ International Ltd, Padstow

To Roger, Dan and Sally

Contents

List of Figures

List of Tables

Preface

In the United Kingdom, career advice, support and counselling are provided in a range of contexts by practitioners from diverse backgrounds. Traditionally, young people had greater access to help with career decision making than adults, through the provision of careers services within secondary, further and higher education. More recently, changes in the employment context have led to a recognition that adults will increasingly need help in managing their careers, and there is now a greater range of provision available within both the public and private sectors.

This book is designed to help those who provide career support, in whatever context, to develop a sound understanding of the theoretical and conceptual base of their work. Until now, career practitioners in the UK have had to rely on American texts, and this volume provides a much-needed British perspective, whilst also covering US literature. It is not a 'how-to-do-it' manual, nor is it an 'all-you-need-to-know' book; at various points readers are guided to other publications containing more in-depth discussions of particular issues. However, it does attempt to bridge the gap between theory and practice by discussing the practical implications of the theories and models discussed. It also takes a critical, research-based stance, and it is very much hoped that its readers will be inspired to read further in the field and to develop a reflective and critical approach to their practice throughout their working lives, perhaps by carrying out their own research.

The volume addresses particularly the needs of students undergoing initial training in career guidance, career counselling or career coaching, and the needs of experienced career and human resources practitioners wishing to keep abreast of the intellectual base of their field. It also provides specialist material for other audiences, for example masters and diploma students in occupational psychology, business and management and applied social sciences, and those working towards professional qualifications, such as occupational psychology chartership and membership of the Chartered Institute of Personnel and Development.

The Introduction begins by defining terms, outlining the provision of career support, and then discussing the current employment context in which careers are experienced. The main body of the text is divided into two sections. In Part I, Chapters 1–4 focus mainly on theory and research and how these inform practice. Career counselling draws on two principal bodies of theory: those concerned with how career decisions are made and how people develop and manage their careers; and those concerned with how to intervene in these processes. Accordingly, Chapters 1 and 2 discuss theories of career decision making and adult career and personal development, while Chapter 3 addresses counselling theories. In Chapter 4, we discuss how career counselling has been evaluated and some of the findings from this research. Part II is more concerned with practice itself, particularly skills, tools and techniques. Chapter 5 outlines a process model of career counselling and some of the skills used. Assessment tools and techniques are introduced in Chapter 6, and the use of career information is discussed in Chapter 7. There are now hundreds of websites offering help with career planning, and Chapter 8 explores some of the issues raised by the use of the internet in career counselling, as well as by the use of computer-aided guidance systems. Lastly, in Chapter 9, some of the ethical issues in providing career counselling are examined.

The material in this book has been adapted and developed from material originally produced for the Masters programmes in Organizational Psychology and Human Resource Management by distance learning offered by the University of London External programme (www.londonexternal.ac.uk) and I am grateful to the University for allowing this material to be included. I am also grateful to those who have commented on drafts of the book, particularly Roger Fry, Tony Watts, Peter Yang and students on the Birkbeck Masters programmes in Career Management and Counselling, Occupational Psychology and Organizational Behaviour.

Acknowledgements

Every effort has been made to trace all the copyright holders, but if any have been inadvertently overlooked the publishers will be pleased to make the necessary arrangement at the first opportunity.

Figure 1.1
From Holland, J.L. (1985). *Making vocational choices: a theory of vocational personalities and work environments* (2nd ed.). Published by Allyn and Bacon, Boston, MA. Copyright © 1984 by Pearson Education. By permission of the publisher.

Figure 1.2
Reprinted from Lent et al. (1994). Toward a unifying social cognitive theory of career and academic interest, choice and performance. *Journal of Vocational Behavior, 45,* 79–122. Copyright © 1994, with permission from Elsevier.

Figure 2.1
Adapted from Erikson, E.H. (1959). Identity and the life-cycle. *Psychological Issues, 1,* 1–171. Used by permission of International University Press, Inc.

Figure 2.2
Reprinted from Super, D.E. (1980). A life-span, life-space approach to career development. *Journal of Vocational Behavior, 16,* 282–98. Copyright © 1980, with permission from Elsevier.

Figure 2.3
Hall, D.T. & Chandler, D.E. (2005). *Psychological success: when the career is calling,* p. 158. Copyright © 2005 John Wiley & Sons Limited. Reproduced with permission.

Figure 5.1
Ali, L. & Graham, B. (1996). *The counselling approach to careers guidance,* p. 63. Copyright © 1996 Routledge. Reproduced with permission.

Table 1.1
Adapted from Rodger, A. (1952). *The seven-point plan.* London: NIIP.

Table 1.2
Adapted from Bedford, T. (1982). *Vocational guidance interviews: a survey by the careers service inspectorate.* London: Careers Service Branch, Department of Employment.

Table 2.1
Adapted from Levinson, D.J., Darrow, D.C., Klein, E.B., Levinson, M.H. & Mckee, B. (1978). *The seasons of a man's life.* Copyright © 1978 by Daniel J. Levinson. Used by permission of Alfred A. Knopf, a division of Random House, Inc.

Table 5.2
Reprinted from Law, B. & Ward, R. (1981). Is career development motivated? In A.G. Watts, D.E. Super, & J.M. Kidd (Eds.), *Career development in Britain.* Cambridge: CRAC.

Table 7.1
Reprinted from Hirsh, W., Kidd, J.M. & Watts, A.G. (1998). *Constructs of work used in career guidance.* Cambridge: National Institute for Careers Education and Counselling.

Introduction

At the start of a book like this, it is common for the author to define terms. This is not as easy as it sounds, not least because practitioners see career counselling and other types of one-to-one career support in different ways. This introductory chapter considers the nature of career counselling, its provision in the UK, and the employment context within which it operates. Before reading on though, you may like to reflect on your own definition of career counselling and write it down.

How far is your definition confined to the concerns people have at work? Have you included broader personal concerns that may impact on work, such as balancing work and family roles? Does your definition focus only on making decisions about career moves? Or does it cover helping people cope with other issues, for example adapting to a new job? And to what extent does it cover career-related concerns in later life as well as initial career choices?

In practice, the issues that career counsellors are called upon to help their clients with are extremely wide ranging. Moreover, the problems clients present career counsellors with often overlap with deeper personal concerns, and as the counselling process unfolds these emerge, complicating the initial picture. Any definition of career counselling, therefore, needs to be broad enough to reflect these features of the process, and accordingly the definition offered here is as follows:

> A one-to-one interaction between practitioner and client, usually ongoing, involving the application of psychological theory and a recognised set of communication skills. The primary focus is on helping the client make career-related decisions and deal with career-related issues.

This definition focuses on work, but it also acknowledges the interdependence of work and non-work concerns.

Career counselling is not just about decision making. Although work and educational choices are likely to be important issues for many clients, many will also need help in dealing with the frustrations and disappointments of redundancy and unemployment, with managing relationships with other people at work, with decisions about whether to return to study or to work, with finding ways to balance different life roles, and so on.

Examples of the concerns which clients may bring to the career counsellor are:

- I've just left university with an arts degree. What does this qualify me for?
- I would like to work for myself, but it's a big step leaving the security of a monthly salary and a pension scheme.
- I want to spend most of my time doing voluntary work. But I also need to think about how to make ends meet.
- I want a job where I don't want to bring work home. Perhaps I should change direction completely.
- I've been out of work for three years and I don't even get job interviews any more. Perhaps I should resign myself to retirement.
- I've spent 15 years bringing up a family. How can I build up the confidence to return to work?
- My employer is making more and more demands on me. How can I be more assertive, and tell her how I see things?
- I've just left school and my mum wants me to start applying for jobs.

These examples show that clients can be of any age, and at any stage in their careers. Moreover, it is clear that they may need help with decisions about jobs, with managing their work responsibilities in relation to other aspects of their lives, or with finding information about career opportunities. Also, many of these presenting problems may mask deeper emotional issues which will not become apparent until later. It has also been noted how often interpersonal issues emerge in the course of career counselling (e.g. Nathan & Hill, 2006) – including problems with dealing with people in authority, lack of confidence in managerial roles and conflict with peers – and some career counsellors offer a service specifically to help clients address relationship issues at work.

What all this suggests is that career counsellors need the knowledge and skills to help clients with these broader concerns, and with the emotional components of career development. One might argue therefore that career counselling should be seen as an *extension* of therapeutic counselling. As Gysbers, Heppner and Johnston (2003) suggest, career counselling belongs in the general category of counselling because it has the same features that all types of counselling possess. It differs from therapeutic counselling, however, because the problems clients present with often concern career development. Also, psychological assessment techniques are used more frequently.

Many writers have called for more integration of career and therapeutic counselling. Blustein and Spengler (1995), for example, call for a 'domain-sensitive' approach where 'interventions are not based on discrete or arbitrary distinctions between treatment modalities but are determined by the unique attributes of each client's history and presenting problem' (Blustein & Spengler, 1995: 318). The aim of any intervention, they argue, should be to improve adjustment and facilitate development in both career and non-career domains. Practitioners should be free to focus on a range of client experiences as a means of furthering understanding and helping the client.

The terms career counselling and therapeutic counselling seem to be useful as ways to organise theory and research, but are not as helpful when seen as implying different types of interventions and techniques. Herr (1997) takes this view, arguing that career counselling is best thought of as a 'continuum of intervention processes', ranging from facilitating self and occupational awareness, exploring opportunities, developing career planning skills, helping with stress reduction, working with indecisiveness and addressing work adjustment. All these require a fusion of career and therapeutic counselling techniques.

In the UK, career counselling and therapeutic counselling have traditionally been viewed as distinct professions. These distinctions still remain, even though career practitioners often use counselling skills in their work. Many career practitioners describe their activities as 'career guidance'. This term has been used in different ways over the years, but it is often employed as an umbrella term to describe the various potential elements in the provision of career support, including group work, information-giving, teaching, self-help activities and assessment, as well as career counselling.

Because of the ambiguities in the term guidance, the term 'career support' will be used throughout this book to refer broadly to the help provided to individuals in planning and managing their careers. This covers all of the above activities, including career counselling.

Given the dramatic increase in the popularity of executive, career and life coaching, it is worth summarising the differences and similarities between career counselling and these activities. The main difference is that coaching, whether the focus is on performance or development, is usually more goal-directed, helping individuals develop action plans for change. The techniques used are often based on models of learning and behaviour change, such as cognitive behaviour therapy. Coaches engage in a range of activities, depending on the needs of their clients. These may include business planning, balancing work and personal life, developing job-related skills (commonly leadership skills) and problem solving. Career coaches may help clients develop career planning and career management skills, but the process of coaching tends to focus on the present, rather than address the impact of past experiences on present functioning, as some career counsellors do. Career coaching, therefore, may be a component of career counselling.

Provision of Career Support

In the UK, a wide range of public and private sector agencies provide career counselling and career support generally. The type of service offered varies considerably, however, from one short interview to in-depth assessment and counselling in sessions spanning several weeks or months. Practitioners working in the field have a range of different qualifications, and some have none. What follows is a brief outline of the services currently available. (A more detailed description of provision is given in a report by Watts, Hughes and Wood, 2005.)

There are three main types of provision in the UK: education/training based; employment based; and 'independent' (Watts & Sadler, 2000). Despite increased opportunities for life-long learning and more job mobility, most state-funded career services operate for young people making the transition from education to work. The public money invested in providing career support to adults has been relatively limited. The main types of provision are as follows.

Education and training-based career support

The provision of career support within educational settings varies in different parts of the UK. In England, all secondary school (aged 11–18) and most further education students (aged 16 upwards) have access to Connexions, formerly the Careers Service, which is funded by the Department for Education and Skills. (Independent schools, however, tend to use independent providers of career support, for example, the Independent Schools Careers Organisation.) Connexions aims to provide an integrated service to those between the ages of 13 and 19, giving every young person access to a 'personal adviser', whose role includes providing support for a range of personal matters, as well as career issues. However, services for part-time students are more limited than those for full-timers. Many schools and further education colleges also have their own careers specialists, who may be involved in career education as well as individual career support.

The introduction of the Connexions service has been criticised, however. In particular, it has been argued that there is a risk of career support in schools being marginalised within its range of provision. This is because the pressing nature of the personal problems of a minority of pupils may lead to personal advisers spending a large amount of their time on these problems, at the expense of the support needed by all students on career related matters (Watts, 2001). At the time of writing, the signs are that Connexions is unlikely to continue in its current form.

Provision is somewhat different in other parts of the UK. In Scotland and Wales, for example, all-age services have recently been introduced.

In all parts of the UK, students in higher education and recent graduates are able to use the careers advisory services in their institutions. The service normally includes individual interviews for those who want them, but there has recently been a strong trend towards self-help activities, particularly with the introduction of computer-aided guidance systems, such as Prospect Planner, which helps students assess their interests, values and skills, retrieve information on opportunities and learn decision-making skills. Careers advisers in higher education have a wide range of employment and training backgrounds, and this is likely to affect the approach they take to individual interviewing, particularly the amount of emphasis given to advice and information as opposed to career counselling.

With regard to provision within vocational training, government-funded schemes for young people and adults have often incorporated career support, usually emphasising assessment rather than career counselling.

Employment-based career support

Partly in response to the need for employees to become more flexible and self-reliant in their career development, many large organisations offer support to individuals in their career planning. Career counselling is offered by some organisations, but other initiatives are more common, for example, development centres, coaching and mentoring schemes, and pre-retirement support. These services are more likely to be offered to professional, technical and managerial staff, although some employers have extended them to the wider workforce, often as part of employee development programmes. Some organisations and professional institutes – for example, the armed forces and the Law Society – also provide career support to their employees and members.

'Independent' career support

The main types of services provided independently from educational institutions and employers include those offered by Connexions, the Department for Work and Pensions, the Learning and Skills Council, learndirect and the private sector. The Connexions Service, as well as providing career support and placement services to students, is also required to provide these services to young people up to the age of 19. Many Connexions services are also involved in managing provision for adults, under separate contracts.

The Department for Work and Pensions New Deal programme offers programmes for the unemployed involving job search sessions, access to the internet and help with writing CVs. Also, the Jobcentre Plus service provides advice on jobs and benefits.

Adult Information, Advice and Guidance (IAG) is available to all adults throughout England, although services vary from area to area. Services are funded by the Learning and Skills Council and delivered via 'next step' partnerships: partnerships may involve higher or further education careers services, private sector providers, voluntary bodies or trade unions. Advice and information about education and training opportunities is also available from learndirect, via its call centre helplines and its website.

Many adults seeking career counselling turn to fee-charging services within the private sector, partly because of limited provision by employers and public sector providers. Many of these agencies are staffed by psychologists or professionally trained career counsellors, though since there is no legislation controlling their operation there is no guarantee that the staff have any relevant training or experience. Most offer psychometric testing and feedback, a series of counselling sessions and access to careers information, and some also provide help with job hunting, CV writing and interview practice. Increasingly, some private-sector career counselling services are marketing themselves as career coaching or career consultancy services, partly to emphasise that the process does not assume some kind of pathology.

Outplacement agencies offer help to employees facing redundancy. A comprehensive service will involve activities similar to those offered by independent career counselling services, though often with more emphasis on emotional support to cope with the trauma of redundancy. Few services employ staff with any significant amount of training in counselling, however. Clients are usually companies, rather than individuals, and outplacement is often offered to employees as part of an overall redundancy package to senior staff. In cases where lower-level staff are offered a service, it may be rather different from the one-to-one programmes offered to executives: support is more likely to be group-based and there will be less in-depth psychometric assessment (i.e., the use of psychological tests and inventories). An important part of the service generally, however, is likely to be job-search: many services base their marketing on how quickly their 'candidates' become re-employed.

In the UK, in a context of more fluid career structures, more career counselling services for adults are particularly needed. Also, greater support is needed for those reaching retirement.

This brief overview of the provision of career support gives some indication of the diversity of roles and work settings through which career counselling and support are offered. In addition, a distinction can be made between those practitioners who have a clearly defined role as a provider of career counselling or career support, and those who use career support and career counselling skills within other roles. Examples of the latter are human resource managers, teachers and lecturers, health workers and social workers.

The Concept of Career

Writers in this field use the term 'career' in quite specific ways, and different writers each have their own viewpoint. Those working in the field of labour economics, for example, have a different focus and a different interpretation of the term from counselling psychologists. They use different methodologies and languages to study careers, and rarely read each others' publications. At the same time, the term 'career' is an everyday term used by lay people, so there is much potential for confusion when we study careers.

The definition of career used here is that employed by Arnold (1997: 16): 'the sequence of employment-related positions, roles, activities and experiences encountered by a person'. Arnold's definition implies that some aspects of career are objective, in that they may be observed and defined publicly, and other aspects are more subjective, best understood in terms of the individual's specific experiences. People's experiences of careers over their life course reflect their changing needs, values, aspirations and attitudes towards work. Other important features of this definition are, first, the breadth of positions implied in the term 'employment related' (self-employment is included, for example, as are educational courses which are employment related); and secondly, the intentional omission of any reference to specific types of occupation or increasing status over time.

Individual careers emerge from the interaction between individual agency and experience on the one hand, and the constraining and enabling forces of the social context on the other. This view has important implications for career counselling: helping clients become more aware of their abilities, interests and work values is not in itself sufficient for effective career planning; they need also to be helped to 'decipher the career rules at work' as they explore opportunities over the course of their lives (Bailyn, 1989).

Career theory provides an analysis of work situations that emphasises several characteristics: the study of both individuals and institutions; and the properties of 'emergence' and 'relativity' (Arthur, Hall & Lawrence, 1989). The focus on both individuals and institutions reinforces the point made earlier in that both the person and the setting in which work is performed are considered. The setting may be a public sector, private sector or voluntary organisation, or, to take a broader view, it may be a professional association or trade union of which the individual has membership. Emergence and relativity are concepts which describe time and 'social space' respectively. The property of emergence suggests that we need to consider how work experiences change over time, according to a person's 'life stage' or 'career stage', for example, and how organisations should adapt their career management practices to take account of changes in individual needs. Taking account of relativity or social space helps us consider the worker role within a range of non-work roles, for example parenting. As we examine various career theories in this chapter and those that follow, we will see how some focus more on some features and some on others.

It is useful to make a distinction between career theories and career counselling theories. As we have suggested, the former are concerned with how individuals experience their careers, how they make career decisions, and the environments in which careers are made. The latter focus on how best to intervene to assist individuals in their career development: they provide a basis for action. To put it another way, career theories are concerned with what is; career counselling theories are concerned with what might be (cf. Watts, Law & Fawcett, 1981).

Swanson and Fouad suggest that a theory is 'a series of connected hypothetical statements designed to explain a particular behavior or set of behaviors' (1999: 3). As such, career and career counselling theories offer a framework within which clients' experiences and behaviour can be understood, and help in the development of hypotheses about what other experiences and behaviours might follow. As we shall see, however, some are more successful in this respect than others. At a more basic level, theories provide counsellors and clients with concepts to organise their thoughts about career behaviour and career interventions. For example, developmental theories provide a language of life roles and life events, which can be easily shared by clients and counsellors.

Clearly, career counselling theories have to take account of career theories, and over the last 50 years or so the primary goals of career counselling have shifted, in line with changing views about career development and about careers themselves. In the UK at the beginning of the twentieth century, simple 'matching' models provided the conceptual base for the so-called 'scientific guidance' provided by the Juvenile Employment Bureaux of the 1920s and 1930s. Assessments of abilities and interests, sometimes using psychometric test results, led to recommendations about jobs and occupations. It was not until the 1960s that these approaches began to be augmented and to some extent replaced by models derived from developmental theories of careers. This led to more emphasis on helping individuals with the process of decision making, rather than just its outcome. In other words, the focus shifted from making wise decisions to making decisions wisely (Katz, 1969).

The Career Context

There is a widespread view that there are no jobs for life any more. It is argued that technological, social and institutional developments have substantially altered the demand for labour. As a consequence, people are now much more mobile between employers (e.g. Arthur, Inkson & Pringle, 1999; Sennett, 1998). It is also suggested that more employees are employed on part-time and temporary contracts (Storey, 2000).

But how far have careers really changed in this way? Employment statistics from Quarterly Labour Force Surveys show that between 1986 and 2004 the numbers of people working with the same employer for 10 or more years stayed much the same: in 1986 the percentage was 29 per cent and in 2004 it was 29.9 per cent of the workforce. Furthermore, the September to November 2004 Labour Force Survey showed that 70.9 per cent of those currently in employment had been with the same employer for longer than two years, and 48.6 per cent had been with them for longer than five years.

Also, it seems that certain groups of workers are staying in their jobs longer. Doogan (2001) has shown that increases in long-term employment are particularly marked in sectors as diverse as public administration, fishing, construction, financial services and manufacturing. So the sectors that have contributed to the increase in long-term employment are found across a whole range of industries and in both private and public sectors.

Increases in rates of long-term employment are evident in both shrinking and expanding industries. For example, manufacturing has downsized, but it also shows an increase in the level and rate of long-term employment. So job shedding seems to be happening alongside labour retention. Doogan's work also shows that long-term employment is higher in skilled, managerial and professional groups (42 per cent of managers and 38 per cent of professionals have been with their employers for more than ten years).

It would appear, therefore, that there was a rise in long-term employment over the 1990s in higher status, higher skill groups, and this is somewhat at odds with many contemporary accounts of how careers are changing. Of course, it may be the case that some of those who remain with the same employer are being mobile in another sense, by moving into different functions or occupations, and we need to know more about this.

With regard to the proportion of employees occupying permanent jobs, statistics show that roughly the same proportion of those in employment were in temporary jobs in 2003 as compared to 1993 (McOrmond, 2004). Other work shows that there was a decline in the proportion of employees working on fixed-term contracts (contracts lasting for between one and three years) in the 1990s. In 1992 those employed on these contracts amounted to 5 per cent, whereas in 2000 only 2.8 per cent were (Taylor, 2003).

In spite of these figures indicating relative stability, there is some evidence that people do appear to feel insecure about employment. Various surveys carried out in the late 1990s showed that between one quarter and one third of their respondents felt they might be made redundant in the near future (e.g. Burchill et al., 1999). There is less consensus on these statistics though. Findings from the ESRC Future of Work Programme showed that only 1.5 per cent said that they expected to lose their job over the next year as a result of the closure of their place of work (Taylor, 2003). This contrasts with 2.2 per cent who expected this in 1992.

To the extent that job insecurity is felt, Doogan (2001) has an interesting argument about why this might be the case. He suggests that it is because of the greater exposure of the workforce to market forces over the last 15 years or so, and a growing *awareness* of labour market instability. Also, the symbolic importance of job gains and losses is highly imbalanced – we hear more about losses than gains, for example – so that public attention is drawn unevenly to particular changes. In the public sector in particular there has grown a 'manufactured uncertainty' that has accompanied the introduction of market forces (for example, separation of purchasing and provision of services, institutional fragmentation and globalisation of public services). In the private sector, waves of mergers and acquisitions, buy-outs and sell offs have generated widespread concern about corporate restructuring.

So it may be that changes in the wider social and economic circumstances have generated anxiety and insecurity, and, as Doogan (2001) argues, this is quite useful for employers and the government, as it serves to 'discipline' the workforce who may come to expect that permanent employment contracts are harder to come by, and that the state is less likely to protect them. In the long term then, they are more likely to accept these conditions.

Another notable feature of the data from employment surveys is that employees' job satisfaction has declined since the early 1990s, particularly in relation to hours of work and the amount of work people are expected to accomplish (e.g. Taylor, 2003). Helping people with problems arising from work intensification and job dissatisfaction seem likely to become an increasing part of the career counsellor's role in the future.

Boundaryless careers?

Connected with ideas about greater mobility is the notion of the 'boundaryless' career (Arthur & Rousseau, 1996), which emphasises the ways that careers are becoming, arguably, increasingly independent from organisations and from traditional job boundaries between specialist functions and skills. The idea of boundaryless careers has led to calls to focus more on subjective careers and how people experience their more fragmented working lives, and it also helps us attend more to the interface between work and non-work.

It does seem to be likely that there is more interorganisational collaboration and more cross-functional working within organisations, and this has reduced the rigidity of conventional boundaries within and between employers. Also there are wider economic trends which are having the same effect, for example, the breaking down of borders in countries within the European Union with the move to a single currency. But it is debatable how far these changes have led to the widespread experience of more boundaryless careers, as the mobility statistics suggest. For many, employment remains bounded within an organisation.

Other writers have argued that careers are becoming more 'protean' (or person-driven) at the expense of the social context (Hall & Mirvis, 1996).

This could be seen as challenging ideas of boundarylessness, as one could argue that boundaries are being redrawn by individuals redefining their career identities. But it seems unhelpful to talk about purely person-driven careers, as different organisational cultures will set their own new boundaries and we have to consider the role of selectors who are also contributing to setting new boundaries to career identities. It has been argued, for instance, that with the shift to mass higher education, credential inflation is leading employers of graduates to adjust their selection criteria, favouring those with particular types of social and cultural capital, for example, membership of interpersonal networks, interpersonal skills and social confidence (Brown, 1995).

It seems clear that we need to understand more about the forces that create boundaries and encourage individuals to challenge them. It appears that social class is still a powerful boundary. Life chances are just as dependent on social background today as they were decades ago. Currently, about four-fifths of young people from managerial and professional backgrounds enter university, compared with only one in six from non-skilled manual backgrounds (Roberts, 2005). Gender is also still a factor in labour market participation. In most western countries women earn less than men for the same or similar job and experience vertical and horizontal labour segregation (Humphries & Dyer, 2005).

As well as these long-standing boundaries, there are new boundaries to contend with. Access to childcare is one. And we need to understand subjective career boundaries: how people make sense of their place in the world. Boundaries between various discourses of careers (ways of talking about them) help people make sense of their experience: the bureaucratic discourse, for example, is still dominant in many people's expectations, despite the delayering and reorganisation that has taken place in many organisations.

Summary

In this short introductory chapter, we discussed some definitions of career counselling, what it might involve, and its relationship to therapeutic counselling and psychotherapy. Career counselling possesses many of the same features and techniques as therapeutic counselling, and it was suggested therefore that it is best viewed as an extension of therapeutic counselling. A wide range of career support and counselling services exists in the UK, but more provision is needed, particularly for adults.

In the second half of the chapter, the term 'career' was defined and discussed. Career theories and career counselling theories were distinguished, and changes in the aims and goals of career counselling over the last half century were discussed. The argument that careers are dramatically changing was examined. In contrast to the views of some writers, job tenure in the UK remains fairly stable, although it is clear that people feel more insecure about their employment. Also, although careers are becoming more 'boundaryless' in some ways, new boundaries are appearing which constrain people's career opportunities.

Discuss and Debate

1 Discuss the advantages and disadvantages of viewing career counselling as an extension of therapeutic counselling.

2 List the services providing career counselling and other kinds of career support that you are aware of in your region and nationally, using the three categories:

Education/training-based support
Employment-based support
Independent support

Do you consider that the career support needs of young people and adults are adequately provided for? If not, what additional services are needed, and for whom?

3 In your experience, how far have careers become 'boundaryless'?

PART ONE   Theory and Research

ONE   Theories of Career Decision Making

In this chapter and the next we discuss some of the theories that attempt to describe and explain how careers develop. This chapter covers theories that deal primarily with the ways people make career decisions, and these tend to focus on the initial entry to work. As we shall see, though, some of these theories also include propositions about later career development. First we examine person–environment fit theories, concentrating particularly on John Holland's work. We then move on to look at developmental approaches, Donald Super's theory being the most well-known example. Structural theories are then briefly discussed, before considering theories which use an inter-personal level of analysis to understand career development and deci-sion making. Throughout the chapter the implications of the various theories for career counselling are considered.

Person–Environment Fit Theories

The idea of person–environment fit (or the degree of 'congruence' or 'correspondence' between workers and their environments) has been the main framework for understanding occupational choice and career decision making over the last century. One of the earliest attempts to describe what happens when individuals choose occupations was that of Frank Parsons, who, in 1908, established his vocational guidance agency in Boston, US. The theory which guided his work consisted of three propositions (Parsons, 1909): people are different from each other; so are jobs; and it should be possible, by a study of both, to achieve a match between person and job. The main implication of these statements for career counselling, of course, is that reliable and valid data are needed about individuals and jobs. Over the following decades, these data were gathered in the form of tests of aptitudes and interests, and also analyses of the skill and interest requirements of occupations.

Person–environment fit approaches to career counselling, therefore, emphasise diagnosis and assessment, and the usual outcome is a recommendation to the client on an appropriate course of action. The practitioner is likely to use questionnaires and inventories completed before the interview (or series of interviews) as aids to assessment.

In the second half of the twentieth century, a commonly used framework for diagnosis, assessment and recommendation was Rodger's Seven-Point Plan (Rodger, 1952). This is simply a list of questions to address in the interview, organised under seven headings. The headings and their associated questions are shown in Table 1.1.

For many years, this was the main model used by careers advisers working with school leavers. It has fallen out of use in recent years, however, largely because of its diagnostic and directive nature and its perceived rigidity. However, many practitioners value the *aide-mémoire* provided by the seven headings.

A much more elaborate theory of person–environment fit was developed in the United States by Holland in the 1960s and 1970s. The most recent version of his theory is set out in his 1997 publication (Holland, 1997). It has been labelled 'differentialist' in that it focuses on individual

Table 1.1 Rodger's Seven-Point Plan

Heading	Questions
1 Physical make-up	Has he (*sic*) any defects of health or physique that may be of occupational importance? How agreeable are his appearance, his bearing and his speech?
2 Attainments	What type of education has he had? How well has he done educationally? What occupational training and experience has he had already? How well has he done occupationally?
3 General intelligence	How much general intelligence can he display? How much general intelligence does he ordinarily display?
4 Special aptitudes	Has he any marked mechanical aptitude, manual dexterity, facility in the use of figures, talent for drawing or music?
5 Interests	To what extent are his interests intellectual? Practical? Practical/constructional? Physically active? Social? Artistic?
6 Disposition	How acceptable does he make himself to other people? Does he influence others? Is he steady and dependable? Is he self-reliant?
7 Circumstances	What are his domestic circumstances? What do the other members of the family do for a living? Are there any special openings available for him?

Source: adapted from Rodger (1952: 8–16)

differences, characteristics that distinguish individuals from others. Holland proposed that people seek occupations that are congruent with their interests (defined as preferences for particular work activities). The most important tenets of the theory are that:

- People and occupational environments can be categorised into six interest types: realistic; investigative; artistic; social; enterprising; and conventional.
- Occupational choice is the result of attempts to achieve congruence between interests and environments.
- Congruence results in job satisfaction and stability.

Holland's six types are as follows:

- Realistic – likes realistic jobs such as mechanic, surveyor, farmer, electrician. Has mechanical abilities, but may lack social skills. Is described as: asocial, conforming, hard-headed, practical, frank, inflexible and genuine.
- Investigative – likes investigative jobs such as biologist, chemist, physicist, anthropologist. Has mathematical and scientific ability but often lacks leadership ability. Is described as: analytical, cautious, critical, curious, introspective, independent and rational.
- Artistic – likes artistic jobs such as composer, musician, stage director, writer. Has writing, musical or artistic abilities but often lacks clerical skills. Is described as: emotional, expressive, intuitive, open, imaginative and disorderly.
- Social – likes social jobs such as teacher, counsellor, clinical psychologist. Has social skills and talents, but often lacks mechanical and scientific ability. Is described as: co-operative, empathic, sociable, warm and persuasive.
- Enterprising – likes enterprising jobs such as salesperson, manager, television producer, buyer. Has leadership and speaking abilities but often lacks scientific ability. Is described as: adventurous, ambitious, energetic, sociable, self-confident and domineering.
- Conventional – likes conventional jobs such as book–keeper, financial analyst, banker, tax expert. Has clerical and arithmetical ability, but often lacks artistic abilities. Is described as: careful, conscientious, inflexible, unimaginative and thrifty.

Holland (1985a) set out a hexagonal model of occupational interests where some of the six types are seen as more similar, while others are more distantly related. This model is described in Figure 1.1, with types at adjacent angles more closely related than those at opposite angles.

A number of instruments have been developed to assess Holland's interest types. These include the Vocational Preference Inventory (Holland, 1985b), the Self-Directed Search (Holland, 1985c, and

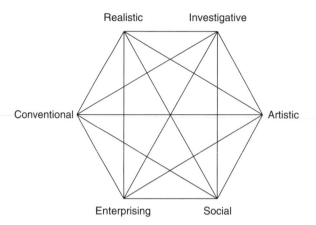

Figure 1.1   Holland's hexagonal model for defining the psychological resemblances among types and environments and their interactions

Source: Holland (1985a)

available at http://www.self-directed-search.com) and the Strong Interest Inventory (Harmon, Hansen, Borgen & Hammer, 1994).

One obvious implication of Holland's theory for career counselling is that practitioners can help clients assess their interests and work environments and understand relationships between them. Simply developing cognitive structures or frameworks with which to view themselves and occupations is helpful for many people. Some career counsellors organise and reference their career and occupational information according to Holland's types, using a three point code corresponding to the most prominent types. This facilitates the process of matching interests and environments.

Holland's main proposition, that individuals make occupational choices that are congruent with their interests, has generally been supported by research (see, for example, Spokane, 1985). However, other work has cast some doubt on his assertion that congruence results in satisfaction and stability (Tinsley, 2000; Tranberg, Slane & Ekeberg, 1993). (The relationship between job satisfaction and congruence, for example, appears to be rather weak, in the order of 0.21.) This may be because people are now more likely to think about what *job* they want, rather than what *occupation* suits them, and that occupational titles are inadequate descriptors of work environments (Arnold, 2004). Furthermore, some writers have questioned the validity of the six-fold model of interests. Prediger (2000), for example, has argued that two dimensions of 'people' versus 'things' should be incorporated into the model.

Subsumed under the umbrella title 'person–environment fit' is a wide range of other theories. These include the Minnesota theory of work adjustment (Dawis & Lofquist, 1984), which focuses on the abilities used at work and the rewards sought from it, and Schneider's attraction-selection-attrition (ASA) model (Schneider, Goldstein & Smith, 1995), which sees fit as a consequence of individual recruitment and selection and subsequent adjustment to the organisation. The ASA model proposes that organisations can be defined by the characteristics of people working in them. Through a process of *attraction*, people are attracted to organisations whose members they resemble; through *selection* they are recruited into posts where they will fit in; and through a process of *attrition* people who do not fit in leave.

Person–environment fit theories have generally found some support (Tinsley, 2000), but the evidence for the validity of Holland's theory is somewhat weaker. This may be because Holland's model oversimplifies the idea of fit; it does not take enough account of the fit between abilities and the demands of work; and it does not pay enough attention to reciprocal influences between individuals and work environments (how work affects individuals and how individuals affect work). As Tinsley (2000) has argued, further research into fit models should take account of conceptual links between interests, values and personality. Other work suggests that models of fit should include abilities also. Ackerman and Heggestad (1997), for example, in a review of studies assessing relationships between abilities, interests and personality, provide evidence for the existence of four clusters of traits across these three domains. These are: social; clerical/conventional; science/maths; and intellectual/cultural. All the clusters include traits across the three domains, apart from the social cluster. The authors suggest that: 'Abilities, interests and personality develop in tandem, such that ability levels and personal dispositions determine the probability of success in a particular task domain and interests determine the motivation to attempt the task' (Ackerman & Heggestad, 1997: 239). This suggests that career counsellors should use frameworks of fit which integrate the domains of abilities, interests and personality.

Present status models

Research into person–environment fit has not given much attention to the probability that certain types of work environment are instrinsically more congenial and satisfying than others. What have been called 'present status' models of relationships between job characteristics and outcomes predict that work environments will affect workers in a uniform way, irrespective of individuals' desires and abilities. Warr (2002) argues that the desirable characteristics of work environments include environmental clarity and feedback, variety, level of pay, physical security, externally generated goals, interpersonal contact, opportunity for skill use, opportunity for control and valued social position. These present status models may be just as valid as person–environment fit models, as well as more parsimonious.

Interests and personality

Researchers have also studied relationships between Holland's occupational interests and other models of personality. Toker, Fischer and Subich (1998) have provided a useful review of this research. There is now some agreement that personality can reliably be described in terms of five broad dimensions (the 'Big Five'): extraversion; neuroticism; openness to experience; conscientiousness; and agreeableness (e.g. Matthews & Deary, 1998). These are defined as follows:

- Extraversion – the extent to which the individual is sociable and outgoing. Extraverts enjoy excitement and may be aggressive and impulsive.
- Neuroticism – the extent to which the individual is emotionally unstable. Those high in neuroticism can be tense and anxious, with a tendency to worry.
- Openness to experience – the extent to which the individual is imaginative and flexible, having a positive, open-minded response to new experiences.
- Conscientiousness – the extent to which the individual is well-organised, planful and concerned to achieve goals and deadlines.
- Agreeableness – the extent to which the individual is good-natured, warm and compassionate in relationships with others.

Toker et al. (1998) reported that the most consistent links between interests and personality are positive associations between openness (being responsive to new experiences and ideas) and investigative and artistic interests, and between extraversion (being outgoing and sociable) and enterprising and social interests.

However, others have argued that personality is likely to make an independent contribution to work outcomes, regardless of fit. For example, Jepsen and Sheu (2003) found that congruence between occupational interests and environments was unrelated to job satisfaction, yet workers in Social, Enterprising and Conventional occupations reported higher satisfaction than those in Realistic jobs. As Hesketh (2000) suggests, one explanation for this is that Social and Enterprising Holland types are likely to be extraverts, that extraverts are on the whole happier than introverts, and therefore extraverts are likely to be more satisfied in any occupation. This may also be because extraverts are more prepared to take steps to improve their jobs to suit themselves. The contribution of personality to career attitudes and outcomes is further supported by a recent study by Bozionelos (2004), which showed that personality plays an important role in career success, particularly intrinsic career success (individuals' subjective satisfaction with career and broader life issues). Those with agreeable personalities displayed greater intrinsic career success, while those high in neuroticism were less satisfied with their careers and with life generally.

The person–environment fit approach to career counselling has often been stereotyped as assuming that the career counsellor's role is simply to offer advice based on expert knowledge of the client and of work opportunities. It has also been criticised as focusing on occupational choice as a one-off event, ignoring the processes leading up to a career decision and later career development. Swanson (1996), however, has argued that these criticisms are unwarranted, and that contemporary versions of person–environment fit approaches see the client as an active agent in the career counselling process. Also, person–environment fit is now more of a reciprocal, ongoing process, where individuals and work environments are in constant interaction. In addition, it is argued that clients can benefit from learning the person–environment fit model as a basis for future problem solving and decision making.

Another criticism of person–environment fit models is that they fail to consider the career counselling process in any detail. The emphasis has been on the information gathered about occupations and individuals – little attention has been given to how that information is used. Rounds and Tracey (1990) have argued that problem-solving and information-processing are inherent within person–environment fit models. For example, theories of problem-solving can be applied to understand better how clients make decisions, how counsellors make diagnoses, and how counsellors might make decisions about the type of intervention most suited to a particular client.

Developmental Career Theories

Differentialist theories like Holland's can be criticised for not taking account of the processes leading up to expressing an occupational preference or making an occupational choice. Developmental orientations attempt to do this in two ways. First, they all take the view that choosing a career and adjusting to work is a continuous process that carries on through life. Secondly, several use concepts from developmental psychology to describe and explain the process of career development. Key concepts in the various models are developmental stages, developmental tasks, career identity and career maturity. We will introduce some of Super's ideas, which are relevant to understanding career decision making, in this chapter and leave discussion of his views on later career development to the next.

Super is the best-known proponent of developmental career theory, with his proposition that career development proceeds through stages. His original stage theory (Super, 1957) portrayed career development as proceeding through five stages: growth; exploration; establishment; maintenance; and decline. A more recent formulation (Super, Thompson,

Lindeman, Myers & Jordaan, 1988) incorporated four stages, and within each, several sub-stages:

- Exploration – crystallisation, specifying and implementing occupational preferences.
- Establishment – settling down in a permanent position and advancing a career.
- Maintenance – holding one's own and innovating in a career.
- Disengagement – deceleration, planning for retirement and living in retirement.

In this model, individuals are acknowledged to 'recycle': those experiencing mid-career change, for example, would be expected to demonstrate some of the concerns of early working life.

In the early stages, Super proposed that the individual gradually develops a realistic self concept and seeks to implement the self concept in an occupation. This is done by matching one's picture of oneself against one's picture of people in occupations that one knows and in which one is interested.

Super's self-concept theory has received some support (e.g. Blocher & Schutz, 1961), though there is evidence that it is the *ideal* self concept that is more important in occupational choice (Kidd, 1984a). Little work has been carried out more recently into the validity of this theory though.

An important notion in Super's theory is that of 'career maturity'. This can be defined as the readiness to deal with the developmental tasks appropriate to one's career stage. The Career Pattern Study, which involved longitudinal research into the career development of 14-year-old boys in the United States (e.g. Super & Overstreet, 1960), led Super (1974) to identify six dimensions of career maturity in adolescents:

- Orientation to vocational choice – the extent to which the individual is concerned with the eventual career choice to be made.
- Information and planning – the specificity of information individuals have concerning career decisions and career planning.
- Consistency of vocational preferences – how far the individual expresses an interest in similar career choices.
- Crystallisation of traits – the amount of progress towards forming a clear self-concept.
- Vocational independence – how far work experience has been gained independently.
- Wisdom of vocational preferences – the individual's ability to have realistic occupational preferences.

Since Super's Career Pattern Study a considerable amount of work has been carried out, particularly in the United States, to assess desirable career attitudes and competencies in adolescence. Much of this work, however, and the measures that have resulted from it, is strongly value-laden, assuming that it is somehow more 'mature' to seek intrinsic rather than extrinsic rewards from work. It also fails to allow for differences between individuals in work salience (the perceived importance of work) (Kidd, 1981).

For example, one of the items in one version of Super, Thompson, Lindeman, Jordaan and Myers' (1981) Career Development Inventory reads as follows:

> JD might like to become a computer programmer but knows little about computer programming, and is going to the library to find out more about it. The most important thing for JD to know now is:
>
> 1   What the work is, what one does on the job.
> 2   What the pay is.
> 3   What the hours of work are.
> 4   Where one can get the right training.

The answer that is keyed to demonstrate most career maturity is 1. In evaluating Super's theory it is important to be aware of its historical origins. Social science theories are products of their times, and their value should be assessed in relation to the social context in which they developed. As we saw earlier in this chapter, prior to the 1950s, concepts of the relationship between individuals and their work were dominated by the static assumptions of differential psychology. Batteries of tests were employed to allocate individuals to jobs and the emphasis was upon matching talents and tasks. In this context, the impact of a developmental approach was monumental.

The strengths of the developmental approach are thrown into sharp relief when viewed from the perspective of career counselling. Until the 1960s, careers advisers and counsellors had the primary aim of diagnosing individuals' attributes and prescribing appropriate occupations. Developmental models, introduced in the UK in the mid-1960s, suggested an educational conception of career support, with emphasis on developing young people's career maturity, particularly awareness of self and opportunities and facilitating decision making.

A developmental approach to career counselling entails attempting to form an accurate and comprehensive picture of the client's career development, and encouraging the client to 'move on' towards a greater awareness of self and situation and greater skills in decision making. Career counselling interventions need to be related to the client's developmental stage. For example, during the early stage of career development the focus will be on educational and occupational decision making and placement in work, while in later stages the emphasis will be broader, taking account of other life-roles (e.g. family responsibilities) in the client's career planning. Super also advocated making probabilistic predictions by employing an historical–developmental analysis for recurring themes and trends and then extrapolating these into the future (Jepsen, 1996).

Super's analysis of the role of the self-concept in career development led to greater attention being given to the subjective perspective of the individual in making occupational choices. Assessment tools are used to facilitate the client's self-understanding, rather than to provide information for the career counsellor's evaluation of the client, as in the traditional person–environment fit approach. The client is an active participant in the selection of assessment tools and the counsellor needs to create a safe environment for discussing the results. Furthermore, occupational information is introduced when the client is ready for it.

The principle that career counselling techniques are more effective when they are in line with the client's developmental stage is reflected in one British framework for describing and evaluating career guidance interviews with young people (Bedford, 1982). Central to this framework is an initial diagnosis of the stage reached by the client at the start of the interview. This is assessed along five dimensions, using the mnemonic FIRST, as described in Table 1.2.

Table 1.2 The FIRST framework

Dimension	Question
Focus	How far has the young person narrowed down options?
Information	How well-informed is the young person about the career options s/he has in mind?
Realism	How realistic is the young person (both in relation to own abilities and the constraints of the market)?
Scope	How aware is the young person of the range of options available?
Tactics	To what extent has the young person worked out the practical steps necessary to achieve his/her career objective?

Source: adapted from Bedford (1982)

The progress made during the interview is also assessed along these dimensions, and each dimension is viewed as contributing cumulatively towards the goal of 'vocational awareness', or being fully prepared for the next career transition.

One strength of the FIRST framework is its simplicity and its potential for use in training. Behaviourally anchored rating scales (BARS) derived from the framework can be applied in evaluating career counselling interventions. (BARS are scales which have points labelled with examples of behaviours signifying different levels of effectiveness on a particular dimension.)

Mignot (2001) argues that one problematic feature of the FIRST framework is the criterion of 'realism'. Assessing the client's realism raises the immediate question of who should be the arbiter of this 'realism': the career counsellor, the client, or, indeed, some other party?

He offers the following example of a career counselling session to illustrate this point (2001: 50).

Jav: Computer programming is for me – information technology – it's where things are going in the future, we're all using them. I surf the net with my mates all the time – and my brother's doing a course – he says it's really good. Anyway, what I want in the future is plenty of money – a decent job, good clothes, a flash car.

Helper: What is it about computers that you like, Jav?

Jav: Computers is hi-tech, it's fast you know – the latest machines work really quick – you can be mobile too – any time, anywhere – work from home, on the train – be your own boss – no-one looking over your shoulder.

Helper: Is there anything that you've said that would be really important for you in the future?

Jav: No-one looking over your shoulder – that would be it. I don't know, it's always been the same – someone's always got to have a dig at you. It was like that at school – I never got it right. When I'm left to get on with it I feel good, more relaxed.

Mignot (2001) argues that the 'uncertain, idiosyncratic and ambiguous' statements that Jav expressed could be obscured by focusing on how far he is being objectively 'realistic'. 'Realism' may in fact be a counter-productive term which encourages premature judgement by the career counsellor. Rather than challenge Jav about his realism, or lack of it, Mignot suggests that he should be helped to elaborate how his ways of viewing the world have significance in career terms. One way to do this is to help him construct a narrative, or story, where 'no-one is looking over your shoulder', and where he is 'feeling good and relaxed'.

In essence, therefore, Mignot is arguing for an *interpretive* view of career counselling, where the social world is seen as relativistic, and can only be understood by being in touch with individuals' own frames of reference. This is in contrast to a *positivist* approach, where objective knowledge is the goal. We will discuss these issues in more detail later.

Structural Theories

Structural theories explain careers in terms of the social environments of individuals. Family background, for example, determines social position in the form of actual and cultural capital (e.g. Bourdieu & Passeron, 1977; Bowles & Gintis, 1976) and this affects educational and occupational opportunities. Structural theories tend to be concerned with the socio-economic status of occupations, and with the segregation of the labour market in terms of, for example, primary and secondary sectors, and along gender lines.

In the UK, a sociologist taking a structural approach offered an assertive challenge to psychological theories of careers, whether person–environment fit or developmental. Roberts (1968) argued that for many young people, occupational choice is myth, since the job attained on entry to work is largely determined by the system of social stratification, not by individual choice. This means that career interventions will have very little impact on individuals' aspirations and destinations.

Roberts (1997) has argued in his more recent work that in most west and east European countries, young people's transitions into work are becoming more prolonged. In the UK, for example, over 30 per cent of school leavers now enter higher education, while in Germany, the typical age when apprentice training commences is 19, and most university students are in their late 20s on graduation.

As transitions have become more prolonged, young people's biographies, Roberts argues, have been 'individualised'. Although this is not an entirely new phenomenon, in many parts of the UK there used to be several main types of employment which most members of broad groups of young people would enter every year. In some parts of the north of England and the Midlands, for example, large numbers of female statutory age school leavers, for example, went to work in the cotton mills. Now, although life chances remain as dependent as ever on social class and educational attainment, this individualisation means that these predictors are exerting their influence in many combinations. And young people are more likely to feel personally responsible for the direction of their future working lives. Adults' careers have become more individualised too, as it has become less common for people to spend their whole working lives in one industry or occupation.

Individualisation, Roberts suggests, has led to greater uncertainty in career development. When groups of young people shared common experiences in their neighbourhoods and schools and then at work, they could look at previous cohorts and glimpse a view of their own futures. Uncertainty has also occurred as a result of the pace of economic, technological and occupational change, which means that the nature of many future jobs is at present unknown.

Career counselling, argues Roberts, can only help young people to operate within the constraints of their particular situations. It 'cannot hasten all young people's transitions, dispel uncertainties, enable individuals to obtain jobs for which they remain unqualified, or alter the specific occupational profiles in particular labour markets' (Roberts, 1997: 352).

Roberts' arguments, of course, operate at the societal level of analysis. As a sociologist, he is more concerned to describe the social context and the limited role of career guidance in the face of structural forces. Nevertheless, he appears to be more optimistic now than in his earlier work about the potential for guidance to help young people cope with more fluid labour markets.

Structural theories are helpful in defining the structural constraints within which career guidance and counselling take place. If we accept the influence of social and opportunity structures on occupational entry, one possible role for career practitioners is to lubricate the mechanisms through which individuals become 'allocated' to jobs. For example, they might work with employers to encourage fairer selection processes. They might also help individuals themselves explore and question the impact of these structural forces.

Social Influence in Career Decision Making

Law's mid-range focus

An attempt at reconciling psychological and sociological approaches to early career development has been made by Law (1981). His 'mid–range focus' sets out interpersonal exchanges within the local community as the prime mediators of career development. Law suggests that: 'the way in which who does what in society is decided is the product of a plurality of interpersonal transactions conducted in local settings, and on the basis of interaction within and between groups of which the individual is a member – the "community"' (Law, 1981: 148).

Law goes on to set out a number of modes and sources of community influence:

- Expectations – refers to the pressures arising from membership of family and community groups.
- Feedback – describes the messages that individuals receive about their suitability for particular occupations and roles.
- Support – refers to the reinforcement of young people's aspirations and of their strengths and weaknesses.
- Modelling – is used to describe the way young people are influenced by example and identification with others in their thinking about work.
- Information – is defined as young people's observations of other people's work habits and patterns.

Law's model is underpinned by a review of previous research into the ways in which young people are socialised into work roles. The propositions about modelling have their roots in social learning theory (Bandura, 1977), where learning is assumed to take place by observing a model and the reward and punishment which follows the model's behaviour. Furthermore, Law's ideas about the ways interpersonal transactions are carried out draw on aspects of symbolic interactionism (Mead, 1934), which assumes that individual identity is formed in interaction with others.

Kidd (1984b) carried out a small-scale study of 15-year-old students' career decision making, and the findings provided independent support for some of the processes that Law described. She also found that help from 'informal' sources of support was much more influential than were the interventions of those who had 'formal' responsibility for career guidance.

Over the last few years there has been something of a revival of interest in understanding the social context of career development. We will discuss this in more depth in Chapter 2. With regard to early career decision-making processes, however, American writers have begun to carry out research into interpersonal influences on career choices. Unfortunately, though, there have been few attempts to build on earlier theory and research. This is one more example of the fragmentation that bedevils this field.

Phillips, Christopher-Sisk and Gravino (2001), for example, interviewed 58 young adults in the US in order to examine the role that other people play in career decision making. Their findings suggested three broad ways in which other people exert an influence in decision making:

- The actions of others. This theme describes how involved other people made themselves with the decider. The categories within the theme form a continuum of involvement with which others engage with the individual. The categories include providing support, information, guidance and criticism.
- The recruitment of others. This theme focuses on how active individuals were in pulling others towards them to help in their decision making. Here, the categories reflect the extent to which the individual demonstrated autonomy. They include relying on others, collaboratively involving others, seeking information about self and others, and others acting as a sounding board.
- Pushing others away. This theme includes instances where individuals exclude others from their decision making. The two categories are: systematic deciding (being methodical) and confident independence (being explicit in excluding others).

Discussing their findings, the authors concluded that the state of an individual's interpersonal relationships may have a strong impact on how they make career decisions. Those with supportive relationships 'play in a different decisional field' from those whose relationships are not as healthy.

Lent, Brown and Hackett's Social Cognitive Career Theory

Social Cognitive Career Theory (SCCT) (Lent, Brown & Hackett, 1994) attempts to explain the development of interests, educational and career choices, and performance and persistence in education and work. The theory suggests that self-efficacy beliefs and outcome expectations both predict academic and occupational interests. Self-efficacy beliefs are defined as 'people's judgments of their capabilities to organize and execute courses of action required to attain designated levels of performance'

(Bandura, 1986: 391). Outcome expectations are seen as 'personal beliefs about probable response outcomes' (Lent et al., 1994: 83). Outcome expectations may be particularly important for those from minority groups, such as ethnic or sexual orientation minorities, since barriers to their goals may be considerable (Fouad & Smith, 1996).

Interests lead to career-related goals, which in turn influence how career-related activities are selected and practised. Activity selection and practice leads to attainments, for example the development of particular skills. At the same time self-efficacy is an independent predictor of goals, activity selection and attainments, and outcome expectancies are independent predictors of goals and activity selection. The model is described in Figure 1.2.

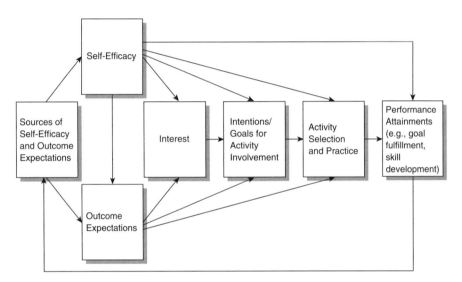

Figure 1.2   Lent et al.'s model of how career interests develop over time

Source: Lent et al. (1994)

Understanding the sources of self-efficacy is particularly important in career counselling, as they can be used to inform the design of career interventions. Bandura (1997) proposes that these sources are:

- Performance accomplishments (i.e. experiences of successful performance of a particular behaviour)
- Vicarious learning or modelling
- Low levels of anxiety
- Encouragement and support from others

It is further suggested that these causes of self-efficacy have their basis in family of origin; other background variables such as social class, gender and ethnicity; and the nature and quality of educational opportunities. As an illustration, Hackett and Betz (1981) suggest that the typical socialisation experiences of girls, as they grow up, might not provide them with the self-efficacy to lead them to develop interests in male-dominated career fields such as science and engineering. And they may be less likely to expect to succeed in these areas than boys.

Research is generally supportive of the assertion that low self-efficacy expectations lead to the avoidance of studying certain academic subjects and related careers (Betz, 2004). Also, low self-efficacy in terms of the process of career decision making appears to be associated with 'floundering', as measured by number of changes of higher education course (Betz & Luzzo, 1996).

Betz (2004) makes a number of interesting suggestions for the use of self-efficacy theory in career counselling. The counsellor's first task is to cover the topic of self-efficacy in early discussions with clients. This involves questions about their beliefs in their competence in career decision making and their abilities. Discussing self-efficacy helps in discovering how far people are unrealistically underestimating their skills and abilities. Measures of self-efficacy for particular areas of occupational interests include the Skills Confidence Inventory (Betz, Harmon & Borgen, 1996). This was developed to measure self-efficacy in relation to Holland's six occupational interests.

If the counsellor and the client agree that there are areas where an increase in self-efficacy may be beneficial, interventions can be planned, based on Bandura's four sources of self-efficacy. For example, in order to increase the likelihood of successful performance the counsellor might help the client build confidence by breaking down large areas of behaviour into more easily learned parts. Similarly, counsellors can identify people who can act as models, either in person, in books or in other media. Betz (2004) gives the example of recommending a book on the life of a female astronaut or scientist as a useful model for a girl considering these occupations. Working on managing anxiety may also be appropriate, using relaxation techniques, for example. Betz's last suggestion, conjuring up an incongruous image for the UK reader, is that counsellors should 'serve as their client's cheerleader', providing encouragement as they try new things.

Another of Betz's (2004) examples is a successful intervention with a client called Richard, a student who was uncertain about the subject he wanted to specialise in. As well as drawing on SCCT principles, it shows how activities outside the confines of the career counselling session can contribute to a positive outcome. Assessment of occupational interests and self-efficacy showed that Richard had only one area of high interest: enterprising. This suggested a career in business management or sales. However, Richard was very low in self-efficacy in relation to these areas, as he lacked social skills and was unassertive. The counsellor decided to try to increase Richard's self-efficacy with regard to enterprising skills and social skills. She convinced him to enrol in a social skills group and a public speaking course, and provided support as he attended these courses. She also taught him relaxation techniques to use when he felt anxious. The outcome was that Richard decided to enrol in a business course and he felt confident that he could succeed. His social skills also improved.

In general, SCCT, as well as other work on interpersonal influences on career decision making, helps us pay attention to the wide range of sources of help and influence that individuals are in contact with. It suggests a role for practitioners as co-ordinators of the human resources which either already influence individuals or could potentially contribute to their decision making. Careers teachers in schools, for example, could invite ex-pupils back into the school to talk about their experiences at work or in higher education. It also suggests that practitioners might intervene to maximise the effectiveness of these resources. A career counsellor could help teachers improve their counselling skills, for example.

Levels of Analysis

To conclude this chapter, it will be useful to take a closer look at the idea of levels of analysis. This is at the heart of the debate about the validity of different theories of occupational choice.

The issue of the relationship between different levels of analysis, or macro and micro frames of reference, crops up frequently in the social sciences. Giddens (1984), for example, describes an 'opposition between theories which emphasize human agency or "action" on the one side, and theories which emphasize "institutional analysis" or "structural analysis" on the other'. He argues for what he calls a 'duality of structure': 'Action and structure stand in a relation of logical entailment: the concept of action presumes that of structure and vice versa'. Concentrating on one to the exclusion of the other limits our understanding of how individuals behave and how social systems work. People do attempt to 'choose' and do use interests, motivations and self-concepts in this process, as Super and Holland argue, but they do this against a background of structural constraints over which they have little control. March and Simon (1958) call this process 'bounded discretion'. This argues for a consideration of both intrapersonal and societal levels of analysis; but what of the others within the hierarchy – the interpersonal and group levels?

It should be noted that the use of the term hierarchy is not meant to imply that some levels of analysis are somehow superior to others. Each level makes a contribution to answering certain types of questions. This point is made here because in the natural sciences quite often the lower levels of analysis are seen as the most fundamental. In physics, for example, explanation in terms of subatomic particles is seen to have special explanatory power.

Reductionism

The process of using concepts from a lower level of analysis to explain events at a higher level is called reduction. This implies that there is a cause and effect relationship between the two levels: processes at a lower level cause the phenomena that we observe at a higher level. To take the reductionist approach to its logical conclusion, it implies that in the end all sciences could be subsumed under a form of physics. In our field, and in social psychology, our understanding of events is enriched by considering explanation at a number of levels. We need to consider what goes on within the individual, as Holland and Super do, and what goes on between people, as social influence theories do, and what happens within groups and organisations and the wider society, as structural theories do. We need all these levels of analysis to produce a comprehensive explanation of behaviour.

To take an example, what determines one 16-year-old's desire to train as a carpenter and her friend's search for work as a hairdresser? Young people's experience is undoubtedly affected by the institutions of society and their cultures. Group pressures may also help explain what happens, but why do some individuals conform to the group's opinion (as in Sherif's (1936) classic experiments on the formation of group norms) and others remain steadfast in their opinions? *Inter*personal explanations, concerned with personal meanings and what people create between them, do not deal adequately with the *intra*personal, for example, beliefs built up from past experience. However, the problem with *intra*personal theories is that, as Sapsford (1984: 81) points out, 'they tend not to be explanations at all, but only descriptions: as soon as we want to ask why the individual thinks, feels or behaves as he or she does, what led up to it, then we are working at one of the other levels.'

Summary

This chapter dealt with theories which attempt to explain early career decision making and the entry to work. Four broad types of theories were discussed: person–environment fit; developmental; structural; and social influence theories.

Holland's work is the most well known of the person–environment fit theories, and his model of occupational interests has been extremely influential in career counselling. Traditionally, this approach was seen as emphasising assessment and expert advice, but more attention is now given to understanding the interaction between the individual and the environment in which careers are played out.

Super's work was discussed as the most important example of developmental career theories. Super proposed that career development proceeds through stages, as individuals attempt to implement their self concept in making an occupational choice. Career counselling, therefore, needs to be related to their developmental stage. Where assessment is used, more emphasis is placed on the client's role in selecting assessment tools, and on their self-understanding, rather than giving expert feedback.

Structural theories focus on individuals' social environments as determinants of the type of occupation they enter, and the work of Roberts is one example. Their main contribution to career counselling lies in the way they describe the structural constraints within which career development takes place.

Social influence theories describe the role other people play in career decision making. Law and Phillips et al. have suggested several ways that others exert an influence on young people's career preferences and choices. Social Cognitive Career Theory, as developed by Lent et al., sets out a key role for self-efficacy in the development of career goals, and a principal source of self-efficacy is social learning (learning through interacting with others). These theories suggest various activities for career counsellors, for example, drawing on other people as sources of help, and using activities outside the counselling session itself to assist their clients.

The final section of the chapter used the concept of levels of analysis to further understand the differences between the theories discussed.

Discuss and Debate

1 Is career maturity a useful concept? If so, what are its main characteristics?
2 How far do you think structural factors (for example, social class and inequalities in educational and occupational opportunities) act to inhibit mobility at the present time?
3 Which of the models of early career development described in this chapter make most sense in explaining the career choices you have made? Why?

TWO Theories of Adult Career Development

The theories and models we have discussed so far have been mainly concerned with the behaviour and attitudes of young people entering the world of work. Models of adult career development focus on career experiences throughout working life, and in this chapter we will examine some of the theories and frameworks which have implications for career counselling. The first part of the chapter deals with theories of personal development, and stage theories of the life course are contrasted with continuity theories. Ways in which these theories inform our thinking about careers are outlined. The second part discusses some theories of adult career development which have been used to inform the practice of career counselling and career management in organisations. Finally, we consider how far the theories discussed are relevant to individuals from non-western cultures.

Theories of Personal Development

A useful summary of some of the commonly agreed features of personal development is provided by Baltes (1987) in his description of the tenets of a life-span perspective. Development is seen as a lifelong process, and it is multidimensional and multidirectional, in that it occurs in a number of different domains, at different rates and in several different directions. Gains and losses are both experienced, development shows 'plasticity' in that it can be modified, and it is a process which is the outcome of interactions between the individual and the environment. Also, development rates and courses vary across different cultures and historical periods. It should be clear then that there is value in understanding how individuals develop in adulthood, and how this impacts on their working lives.

Stage theories

Many writers on adult development have viewed the course of life as a series of stages, each of which is relatively stable and qualitatively different from others. This notion of stages forms the basis of some well-known theories of child development, for example Freud's psychosexual theory and Piaget's conceptualization of the development of cognitive abilities and moral judgement. Two principal contributions to the life-stage approach to development are those of Erikson (1959) and Levinson, Darrow, Klein, Levinson and McKee (1978).

Erikson's epigenetic theory

Erikson's work focuses on ego development and its functioning and is rooted in Freudian ideas. His approach contrasts with Freud's more deterministic stance, however: the ego is described as the 'inner synthesis which organizes experience and guides action' (Erikson, 1959). Erikson conceived of eight stages of ego development through life, each of which involves an interplay between a pair of alternative orientations. Where the individual resolves each issue successfully, there emerges a 'virtue' or particular quality of ego functioning. Erikson's stages are shown in Figure 2.1 below.

Erikson's theory is *epigenetic*. This means that although each polarity and its emergent ego quality has its particular time of ascendance, it is not restricted solely to that stage. For example, once the capacity for competence has emerged, it is likely to persist through life. Furthermore, the individual should not be thought of as being located at only one particular stage. At any one time, there tends to be an oscillation between different conflicts.

Each of Erikson's stages is set in a social context. The demands of society prompt the tasks associated with the resolution of each polarity. The school-leaver is confronted with identity-related tasks of occupational choice and the new parent is expected to provide guidance to the next generation.

Another aspect of Erikson's approach which meshes well with the conception of careers taken here is his idea of 'triple book-keeping': we can only come to a full understanding of personal development if we view it in interaction with the social context, and with biological development.

Erikson's conception of the stages of ego development was based upon his clinical work as a psychoanalyst. The only evidence that he offers in support of his propositions is from such case studies. Erikson's work might also be criticised for its rather benign view of society. He tends to give little attention to the possibility that the social reality may be repressive or constricting and assumes that being out of step with society is psychologically unhealthy.

Other formulations of the life cycle have been grounded in empirical research. Vaillant (1977), for example, traced the lives of Harvard alumni until they reached 50 years of age, and Gould (1978) carried out a cross-sectional study of a group of middle-class men. Two books aimed at the general reader which describe people's experience of change through the life cycle are those by Sheehy (1976), an American, and Nicholson (1980) who is British. Both of these accounts are based on interviews.

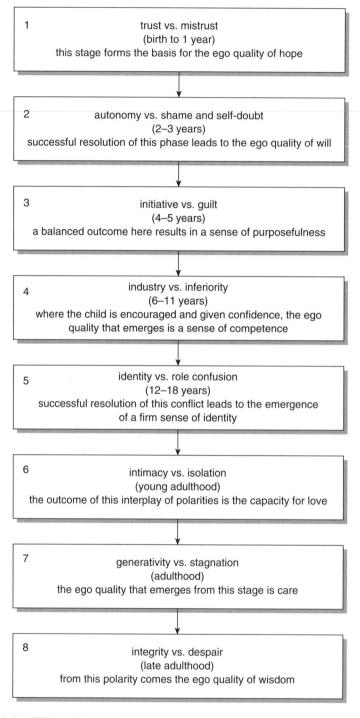

Figure 2.1 Erikson's stages of ego development

Source: adapted from Erikson (1959)

Levinson's model of development

Another well-known piece of research in this area is the work of Levinson, Darrow, Klein, Levinson and McKee (1978) described in the aptly named book *The Seasons of a Man's Life*. This study left out 50 per cent of the population, of course, and that is an acknowledged limitation of his work. In spite of this limitation, Levinson's account makes some important points about development and change which are very relevant to our consideration of careers. We will consider how far his findings might be generalised to women later.

The respondents in Levinson et al.'s study were 40 men aged between 35 and 45 at the start of the research. Four occupational groups were selected for study – industrial workers, executives, biologists and novelists – and ten respondents were chosen from each group. The sample was reasonably diverse in terms of socio-economic background and educational level, but it was biased towards the upper end of the social class spectrum. Data were collected using a biographical interview which aimed to elicit 'life stories' and develop generalisations based on these.

Analyses of the biographies led Levinson and his colleagues to share Erikson's view that the life cycle can be seen as a series of stages or seasons, each with its own character. They delineated four broad and overlapping 'eras', and subdivided each era into a sequence of 'periods' lasting between five and ten years. Within each era there are structure-building periods concerned with establishing and extending what has been attained earlier. These allow individuals to focus on non-work issues, develop work-related skills, and prepare for transition periods which come at the end of each era. This permits review and exploration and prompts movement to the next phase.

A simplified version of Levinson's developmental stages and associated tasks is shown in Table 2.1.

One of the major tasks of early adulthood is to give greater definition to aspirations and visions. Levinson et al. use the idea of 'The Dream' to describe an imagined possibility that provides inspiration and energy. The individual's task is to give the Dream greater definition and to find ways to live it out. In their sample, the biologists and novelists tended to have dreams that were connected with their work. The executives' dreams were more likely to be concerned with their families and social lives. A number of the industrial workers had fantasies about exciting types of work and achievements, but, somewhat depressingly, these had usually faded with the passage of time.

The mentoring relationship is regarded by Levinson as one of the most important in the early adulthood stage. It is most frequently situated in the work setting, where mentoring functions are taken by a boss or senior colleague. The mentor tends to be seen more as an older brother or sister rather than as a parent-figure, and an important aspect of that

Table 2.1 Levinson's developmental stages and tasks

Eras	Stages	Tasks
Early adulthood	Early adult transition (17–22 years) Entering the adult world (22–28 years) Age 30 transition (28–33 years) Settling down (33–40 years)	Following a dream, forming mentor relationships, developing an occupation, forming love relationships
Middle adulthood	Mid-life transition (40–45 years) Entering middle adulthood (45–50 years) Age 50 transition (50–55 years) Culmination of middle adulthood (55–60 years)	Review, revise and modify, individuation
Late adulthood	Late adult transition (60–65 years)	Coming to terms with being old

Source: adapted from Levinson et al. (1978)

relationship is that as the young man's skills increase, the relationship gradually becomes more equal. The mentor may function as a teacher, a sponsor, a host and guide, an exemplar that the young person may seek to emulate, or he or she may simply provide advice and support. Mentoring, then, can involve a range of differing roles; some require the mentor to be in a position of power, others do not.

Little empirical research on Levinson's theory has been carried out, and most of it does not support the links that they propose between age and attitudes. However, there is some evidence that the 'age 30' transition described by Levinson is more disruptive psychologically than later transitions. Wetherington, Kessler and Pixley (2004) studied the 'turning points' or significant changes in life directions experienced by over 700 Americans aged 28–78. The respondents were asked if they had experienced a turning point in the last five years. The most frequent type of turning point involved a work issue, usually a job or career change, and these were more likely to occur around the age of 30. The prevalence of the mid-life crisis may be overstated therefore, and these findings suggest that significant numbers of people may be in need of career counselling in early adulthood, at a time when they may be rethinking an earlier career choice.

Levinson's sample was confined to men and the respondents came from a homogeneous group in terms of social background (western and largely white middle-class males). Another shortcoming of the theory is that, although the study was longitudinal, the four-year time frame is very short in the context of a total life span. With regard to the validity of the findings, it is difficult to tell how far the propositions were explicitly derived from the interview data. The theory evolved through seminars and discussions amongst Levinson's team, and he admits that the personal experiences of the group as well as the data were used in its development.

Women's experiences

Only a handful of studies have examined the generalisability of Levinson et al.'s model to women. In the 1980s Levinson conducted in-depth interviews with 45 female academics, professionals and homemakers between the ages of 35 and 45. The findings of this work were published after his death (Levinson & Levinson, 1996) and these showed, it was argued, that women do progress through the same age-related stages as men, but, not surprisingly, their development is more affected by cultural and social stereotypes and sexism. However, a study by Ornstein and Isabella (1990) examined whether organisational commitment, turnover intention and desire for advancement differed for women of different ages. The patterns of review and reassessment they found were not in line with those suggested by Levinson.

It is clearly possible for women, through their own experience, to assess how far their actual lives fit male-based theories like that of Levinson et al. The danger here, though, as Gallos (1989) points out, is that male-based theories are seen to provide the language and concepts which then become the basis for examining women's lives. These concepts *may* be significant in understanding women's lives, but they may also blind us to other distinctive issues for women. Keele (1986), for example, points to the importance of developing a number of 'weak ties' in lieu of a significant sponsor or mentor, and Gilligan's (1982) view of women's development emphasises the sometimes overriding importance of social relationships and attachments over and above career success. Moreover, for many women, the life course may be related more closely to the family life cycle and the degree of involvement and investment in family roles than to chronological age. So instead of looking to see how far women's experiences depart from those of men, we may need to develop quite separate or different theories to account for female development.

Sekaran and Hall (1989) discuss the way the various roles of parties in dual-career couples develop within the life space, and they attempt to analyse the interactions between career, family and personal life stages and transitions. Sekaran and Hall argue that the young parenthood stage is the most stressful period in the lives of the dual-career couple. This tends to be the time when both partners are expected to make substantial investments in their careers and at the same time the young family is at its most demanding. In the face of this situation, many couples conform to the current cultural expectation: that it is the male partner who focuses mainly on his career, while the woman attends more to the family. These behaviours are reinforced by organisational expectations, where women's decisions to work part-time or to take time off for child rearing are accepted more readily than are men's. In the cases where the couple does decide that the father will be the partner who cuts back on work, these men are often seen by organisations as eccentrics who cannot possibly be serious about their career (Krett, 1985).

Using stage theories

Description of what typically happens is an important first step in theory development, but we also need explanations of why certain things happen. Why do some individuals conform to Levinson's stages, for example, while others deviate from them? How far does Levinson's work provide explanations of our experience?

Perhaps Erikson's and Levinson's schemes are best seen as tools to think with in career counselling. Through reading their work, we may come to be more aware of themes and patterns and the way individuals deal with events. Their ideas may perhaps contribute to *anticipatory socialisation,* helping individuals look ahead to the issues and transitions they may have to face in the future and enhancing the capacity for dealing with development in an autonomous way. Just as important, some of this work goes some way to helping us think about the way social institutions can better accommodate the changing pattern of individual needs through the life-cycle. If we know that certain periods of life tend to be times when many individuals need to review and evaluate their life so far, we can make suggestions about ways in which career counsellors can help people deal with these needs.

Notions of developmental stages and tasks, when applied to organisational careers, inevitably lead to judgements about whether career progress (in whatever sense), or progress through life generally, is on or off schedule. Writers have pointed to the existence of a 'social clock' (see, for example, Schlossberg, Troll & Leibowitz, 1978), which gives us an indication of when and how certain behaviours are expected to occur. There are certain times in adulthood when particular life events usually happen: for example, the age of entry into higher education is usually taken to be the late teens. If our own life seems to be out of synchronisation with these norms, we may experience feelings of uncertainty, inadequacy or anxiety.

Linked to this idea, the age distribution within an organisation forms an implicit *career timetable* and evidence suggests that people use their perceptions of this timetable to determine whether their careers are 'on or off schedule' (Lawrence, 1984). Two judgements are implied in perceptions of age expectations that define normal progress within an organisation:

first, individuals observe the age distribution of those in different levels within their company; and secondly, they judge what range of ages represents normal progress, fast progress and slow progress.

People's perceptions of their own positions are based on these judgements and they therefore contain positive and negative evaluations. Those who see themselves as younger than normal may define themselves as being in the fast track and those who view themselves as older may be concerned that they are getting nowhere. Kanter (1977) calls these two types of managers the 'mobile' and the 'stuck'.

Lawrence (1984) found that those managers who saw themselves as 'behind time' in their careers had more negative attitudes to work than other managers. And the longer the managers remained in the same job, the more likely they were to define themselves as 'behind time'. However, there is no firm evidence from this cross-sectional study to suggest that feelings of being behind time caused negative attitudes. A lack of commitment to work or to the organisation may have led to relative immobility.

If managers' perceptions of themselves as being behind schedule result from infrequent job moves then organisations may be able to alleviate some of the negative feelings experienced by providing alternative job opportunities. It may be that movement itself, rather than upward movement, is what is important. Therefore lateral moves may be just as effective as vertical moves. This may be an important consideration where an ageing workforce lessens opportunities for upward mobility.

Other work has suggested that being off schedule (late or early), in terms of age-specific life events, such as finishing school, starting work and getting married, is related to lower earnings (Hogan, 1980). Furthermore, men and women who are on schedule with major family events, such as marriage and the birth of children, seem less likely to experience career change as a crisis than those who are off schedule (Lawrence, 1980).

An important general question to raise about stage theories like those discussed here is the extent to which it is useful to describe the typical or average experience. The danger is that descriptions of development become prescriptions (for example, we may expect a mid-life crisis and interpret events accordingly). We need to remember too that age in itself causes nothing, and Nicholson has given an illustration of the absurdities to which age-related explanations can be reduced:

> Suppose, for example, you wake up one morning feeling depressed for no obvious reason. There is no need to get alarmed. It is your age that is causing it, however old you happen to be. Two? You are having problems resolving the trust-versus-mistrust psychosocial crisis. Twelve? Puberty is on the horizon. Twenty two? Who would not be depressed by the intimacy-versus-isolation crisis which is alleged to overshadow this period of our lives? Thirty-two? You are in the middle of the first major life review, facing the painful task of deciding whether you have chosen the right partner or job. And so it goes on...through the mid-life crisis, the menopause (male and female varieties), the pre-retirement era, the transition to life without work, and finally the decline through senescence and senility towards the merciful escape offered by the grave. (Nicholson, 1980: 13–14)

Continuity theories of the life course

Much of the discussion of development so far in this chapter has focused on differences between various life stages and the developmental tasks that individuals need to accomplish within these stages. Other writers, however, emphasise stability and continuity over the life course, and the ways in which we 'maintain a continuous sense of who we are and explain our current behaviour and aspirations as in some way connected to what has come before' (Sugarman, 2001: 163).

Atchley's continuity theory

Atchley (1989) distinguishes between external and internal continuity over the life course. Being in familiar environments, taking part in familiar activities, and interacting with familiar people are all evidence of the external continuity that most of us experience. Sugarman (2001) points out that the sequence of roles that we are expected to fulfil over our lives often exemplifies continuity rather than change, and it is often based on accumulated experience and learning. Deciding to change the direction of our career, for example, might lead to warnings from others that we would be wasting all the time and effort we have put in to reaching our current position. Also, we are often encouraged to construct our curriculum vitae to show how our current position is a logical consequence of earlier learning and work experience.

Atchley's (1989) notion of internal continuity involves the maintenance of a persistent sense of our own identity: our awareness of a consistent structure of 'ideas, temperament, affect, experiences, preferences, dispositions, and skills' (Atchley, 1989: 185). This awareness of identity is dependent on a memory of the past which enables the individual to experience continuity, and to see changes in attitudes and experiences to be linked to the past. Continuity, therefore, is not the opposite of change, instead it describes how change happens within a stable context of the individual's past.

It is often argued that because career patterns have become more unpredictable, the need for a greater sense of personal and career identity is now greater so that the individual can develop a satisfying work life. Law, Meijers and Wijers (2002) have set out the main challenges involved in developing career identity as:

Differentiating self from others.
Actively assimilating information into one's own life story.
Acknowledging the good and bad feelings that are involved in managing one's career.
Understanding one's values and purposes in life.

Career counsellors have a role, therefore, in helping individuals with these issues.

Clearly, crises of identity which require the reorganisation of an individual's self-concepts can be extremely distressing. This can happen in cases of serious mental or physical illness, particularly where memory is affected. Apart from these severe conditions, some threats to internal or external continuity may not be unwelcome, and may be seen as part of natural change in the life course. Also, individuals vary in the extent to which they see change as important – Atchley sees optimum continuity as meaning that the person 'sees the pace and degree of change to be in line with her or his coping capacity' (Atchley, 1989: 185).

Narrative theories

Writers taking a narrative perspective on the life course go one step further in their examination of continuity. They emphasise the process of re-interpreting the past in order to develop and maintain a coherent story, rather than just the existence of a memory of a consistent past. The narrative approach to development emphasises what it calls 'emplotment': the process of viewing the self as the main character in a meaningful and productive narrative (Cochran, 1997).

A narrative helps us make sense of our experiences by ordering them in a sequence, and describing them in terms of a theme or themes. Each narrative should have a beginning, a middle and an end.

McAdams (1997) has suggested a way in which individuals can compose their own life narrative by working through an interview schedule with seven sections. These cover, he argues, all the key features of a personal narrative. The sections include describing your life in terms of a sequence of chapters of a book, focusing on eight key events in your life, and considering future 'script', or what will happen next in your life.

Focusing on key events (a particular incident or episode in the past) often provides the most powerful indicator of dominant themes in the narrative, and McAdams suggests the following way of doing this:

Identify eight key events in your life:

1   A peak experience (a high point)
2   A nadir experience (a low point)
3   A turning point
4   Your earliest memory
5   An important childhood memory (positive or negative)
6   An important adolescent memory (positive or negative)
7   An important adult memory (positive or negative)
8   Other important memory (positive or negative)

For each event, describe in detail what happened, where you were, who was involved, what you did, and what you were thinking and feeling. Then reflect on the following questions:

What impact did each event have on your life story, and what does each say about who you are as a person?

Did it change you?

What are the dominant themes here?

Writers taking a narrative perspective on development argue that telling our own stories in this way can be empowering, since it enables us to define actively who we are. However, these stories can be seen as temporary constructions rather than as representing enduring personality traits or behaviours. This implies, of course, that from any set of life experiences more than one story could be told, and also that the narratives we construct about our lives may change. Is the 'truth' of any particular memory relevant? Does it matter if the way the impact of an event is described bears little relation to any 'reality'? We will discuss these issues in more depth in Chapter 3, when we consider narrative approaches to counselling.

Cultural narratives

Not only do we construct and tell narratives about ourselves, we also are the recipients of others' narratives about who we are, and what we might expect. Some of these may be 'imperfect guides' (Cochran, 1997), however. An example is the 'disengagement' narrative that it is normal to withdraw from significant others as we age. Also, cultural narratives can become out of date: for instance the notion of occupational choice as a once-and-for-all decision. Narratives can also conflict. For example, individuals of Asian origin living in the UK may be torn between the eastern narrative that emphasises obligations to family, and the western narrative of self-fulfilment.

As Sugarman (2001) points out, narratives provide a vehicle for understanding the life course in a similar way to the notion of life stages. As we have seen though, the life stage model of the life course has become less tenable now that there are fewer set paths through education and employment. The narrative perspective is more in tune with individualised career patterns and the corresponding importance of individuals becoming authors of their own personal narrative.

Theories of Career Development

We turn now to consider some theories of adult career development which have implications for the practice of career counselling.

Super's life-career rainbow

Super (1980) has used the image of a rainbow to describe the individual's 'life space' and the various roles within it. An example of a 'life-career rainbow' is given in Figure 2.2. The bands in the rainbow represent the different roles a person assumes during the course of his or her life. Breaks in the bands indicate where the individual ceases to play the role, as in the case of the parent who temporarily leaves work to look after a young family. Initially, the life space contains only one role, that

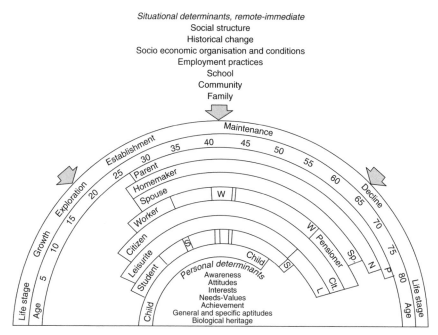

Figure 2.2   Super's life-career rainbow

Source: Super (1980)

of the child, but during adulthood many people experience seven or eight roles, as when a person is employed in an occupation, studying part-time, being a parent, being a partner, maintaining a home, supporting ageing parents and pursuing hobbies. Clearly other roles could be identified, and not all roles apply to all individuals. In addition, the sequencing of roles may vary.

Although much research into Super's theory supports the idea of differences in attitudes and behaviours across career stages (e.g. Pogson, Cober, Doverspike & Rogers, 2003), a lot of this work has been cross-sectional and used age as a proxy for career stage. In addition, the theory's generalisability to women has been questioned (Ornstein & Isabella, 1990). However, Super's life-career rainbow better portrays the experiences of individuals with discontinuous careers than his early work.

One problem with Super's propositions about career development in adulthood is that the processes set out as being characteristic of later stages are discussed only in a very general descriptive way. Unlike the exposition of the earlier stages, there is little attempt at explanation, and it is difficult to formulate testable hypotheses beyond general statements. The theory also fails to address adequately the issue of what happens to individuals once they become employed in organisations.

Another drawback of Super's theory is that it pays little attention to the psychological processes involved in changing jobs and adapting to work environments. We turn now to discuss some work that examines these processes of change and adjustment.

Career transitions and cycles

Nicholson and West (1988) offer the following definition of a work-role transition: 'any move into and/or out of a job, any move between jobs, or any major alteration in the content of work duties and activities'. This definition can include the initial entry into work, moving from one job or role to another, returning to work after a period raising a family or a time of unemployment, or, a substantial change of work tasks and responsibilities without change of job title.

One approach to transitions emphasises the idea that change can often be stressful, and focuses on emotional reactions. Transitions are often seen as generating a predictable cycle of reactions and feelings, and a number of writers have plotted the path of the transition cycle which is set in motion when 'an event or non-event results in a change in assumptions about oneself and the world and this requires a corresponding change in one's behaviour and relationships' (Schlossberg, 1981: 5).

Adams, Hayes and Hopson (1976), suggest seven stages that an individual passes through in any transition period:

- Immobilisation
- Minimisation
- Depression
- Letting go
- Testing
- Searching
- Internalisation

Nicholson (1990) has set out a rather different model of the transition cycle which focuses more on the career-related tasks which need to be carried out at each stage. His four stages are as follows:

1 Preparation – expecting and anticipating change.
2 Encounter – developing an understanding of the new situation.
3 Adjustment – finding ways of coping with the new situation.
4 Stabilisation – becoming settled in the new situation.

During the preparation stage, some anticipatory socialisation takes place before the transition is made, but expectations may not be realistic. At the encounter stage, there is a process of sense-making, and it is here that the change from previous roles occurs. At the next stage, adjustment, personal and role development take place, which usually increases the fit between the individual and the job. At the final stabilisation stage, there is generally increased commitment to the organisation as the individual copes successfully with the new role.

The model emphasises the cyclical nature of career stages: Nicholson calls this property 'recursion'. Undergoing a transition is in itself a preparation for the next one. Furthermore, the cycles may short-circuit each other. Adjustment, for example, may be interrupted by the preparation and encounter stages of a new cycle. In addition, experiences at one stage will strongly influence what happens at later stages. Nicholson calls this 'interdependence'. Inappropriate preparation, for example, increases the challenge of encounter and adjustment. A third feature of the transition cycle is 'distinctiveness'. It has discontinuous stages, each having distinct tasks.

Research is lacking as to the existence of these stages as described, but there has been some attention to individuals' experiences within each stage, and on the organisational processes that help individuals achieve specific tasks within each. For example, Premack and Wanous (1985) found that realistic job previews, which give job applicants (those in the preparation stage) an accurate idea of jobs and employing organisations, do help individuals develop more realistic expectations, and can increase job tenure.

Hall (2002) takes a more psychological perspective to career development, arguing that individuals have greater agency in their career decisions and need to be adaptable and competent learners. He describes how people experience mini-career cycles, which involve sequences of goal-setting and effort leading to objective and psychological success, which produce, in turn, changes in identity (see Figure 2.3)

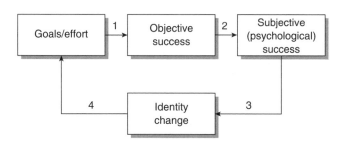

Figure 2.3 Hall's model of psychological success

Source: Hall and Chandler (2005)

Central to Hall's model are the concepts of objective and subjective career success. As Nicholson and de Waal-Andrews (2005) argue, the relationship between these two aspects of career success is at the heart of the most important challenges for theory and research in the field. What constitutes career success is also of critical importance to career counselling, since many clients will enter counselling in the hope of gaining an understanding of how to achieve success and satisfaction at work.

Objective career success consists of observable career outcomes such as hierarchical position in an organisation, status, social reputation, salary and work-related skills. Subjective career success depends on one's values, but may include job satisfaction, career commitment, self-efficacy and moral satisfaction. Although the two types of career success tend to be seen as interdependent (Arthur, Khapova & Wilderom, 2005), much recent careers literature extols the importance of subjective success, given the assumed context of fewer opportunities for advancement up the corporate career ladder. But aspects of objective career success are still important, for example, there is a high correlation between income and satisfaction (Clark & Oswald, 1996). As Nicholson and de Waal Andrews (2005) suggest, individuals need unbiased career support that helps them understand where to invest their effort to maximise the career outcomes they aspire to. This support is all too uncommon in organisations, as advice is often supplied by those who have a vested interest in an individual's choices.

We have seen, then, that viewing the life course in terms of periods of transition and learning leads us away from age-related stages of development and allows us to attend more to the experiences of individuals rather than to normative life events. Arguably, therefore, they have more potential to describe and explain women's careers. As S. Jacobs (1999) points out, women's careers are increasingly variable: they experience a range of diverse and often discontinuous career patterns. She also shows how the female workforce is polarised. Childless women and full-time employed mothers working in relatively high-status, well-paid jobs are at one extreme, and mothers in low-status, badly-paid jobs are at the other. Women are more likely than men to interrupt their careers and transition theories can accommodate this.

This is not to say, of course, that women's common experiences should not be acknowledged. Structural factors, such as gender segregation in the labour market and discrimination, are important features of many women's employment experiences. Fitzgerald and Harmon (2001) have argued, indeed, that matters of equality of pay and opportunity in the workplace are now more important than issues relating to the entry to work. Also, the fact that women are still seen as the primary carers of young children, and often of the elderly, is one of the principal constraints on career development. This was borne out by a recent survey carried out by the Chartered Institute of Personnel and Development, which showed that needing time for family responsibilities and taking a career break were seen by HR practitioners as two of the factors which most negatively influenced career progression (CIPD, 2003). Others have suggested that another common concern that women have is the desire to find fulfilment in relationships with others (e.g. Powell & Mainiero, 1992). We have to take care not to overgeneralise, though. Plenty of men see relationships as important too.

Career management as a social process

Another model of organisational careers which emphasises interdependence, in the form of social interaction, is that of Herriot and

Pemberton (1996). They built on the work of Argyris (1960) and Rousseau (1990) to propose a social process model which defines organisational careers as 'the repeated renegotiation of the psychological contract', based in perceived matches between what each party (the employer and the employee) wants and what the other has to offer (Herriot & Pemberton, 1996: 762). Change is therefore a constant feature of the employment relationship. Communication between employers and individuals is seen by Herriot and Pemberton as essential in managing one's career, and there is some evidence that kept promises on the part of organisations contribute to employees' job satisfaction and their intention to stay with the firm (e.g. Conway & Briner, 2002).

In a similar vein, Kahn (1996) has argued that to the extent to which employees are able to develop meaningful attachments in their organisations, they will use these relationships in managing their careers. It appears that employees draw on a wide range of sources of formal and informal support for their career development, including senior managers, their boss, human resource managers, coaches, and friends and colleagues (Kidd, Hirsh & Jackson, 2004).

The main strength of these approaches is that they encourage us to see career development as much more than sequences of occupational decisions. Rather, they draw attention to the importance of ongoing interactions and negotiations between individuals within social and organisational environments. One implication for career counsellors, and for individuals, is that in order to have a basis for negotiation with employers, individuals need to be clear about their work identities and values (that is, how they view work in the context of other aspects of their life, and what they want from it). Also, negotiation skills are important in career management, and individuals need to recognise their negotiating power. This emphasis on work identities and agentic (self-directed) behaviour is consistent with the writings of those who take a constructivist view of careers (e.g. Cochran, 1997), which focus on how work fits into people's lives, rather than assessing 'fit' between individuals and jobs. The constructivist approach also emphasises the importance of individuals gaining understanding of the context in which their careers develop.

Similar conclusions about the range of career planning and career management skills that will be required in the future have been drawn from debates about the future of work. As we saw in the Introduction, the scenario commonly described is one of short-term contracts, part-time work and 'portfolio' careers. This scenario may be overstated, but the moves already apparent towards greater functional flexibility will mean that individuals will need to be clear about their development needs, more knowledgeable about the way labour markets are heading, and prepared to hone the 'meta-skills' of continuously monitoring self and situation (Kidd & Killeen, 1992).

With the possibility of frequent job moves and the prospect of periods of unemployment, individuals will also need the emotional capacity to cope with uncertainty and insecurity. Many will cope well, of course, and will positively welcome changes of job and employer and the challenge of working with new people. Coping well may also mean having the confidence to challenge exploitative practices in the work place. Career theory has largely overlooked this affective component of career development (Kidd, 1998), although it seems likely that career events produce a broad range of emotions, which can affect the way people approach their work and their careers.

Career development skills

The theories discussed in this section suggest that individuals need a range of career skills and attitudes in a less-certain labour market. In addition certain feelings and emotions will be more adaptive than others. These attributes can be grouped into decision-making skills; career management skills; and career resilience (a term used by London (1983) to describe the persistence aspect of career development). Table 2.2 sets out the main features of each set of attributes.

Table 2.2   Key career development skills, attitudes and emotions

Career decision making (Specific knowledge and skills)	Career management (Identity clarification and meta-skills)	Career resilience (Attitudes and emotions)
Relating self- and opportunity-awareness	Ongoing assessment of values and goals	Confidence
		Hope
	Monitoring and exploring self and situation	Flexibility
Understanding how emotions affect decisions		Self-esteem
	Negotiating	Self-reliance

Decision making involves developing an awareness of career-related opportunities and a sense of identity as an individual and understanding the relationship between the two. This awareness will involve an appreciation of how one's emotions can colour decisions. Career management entails clarifying and assessing on an ongoing basis one's values and goals, monitoring changes in the social context, and using negotiating skills with the gatekeepers of opportunities. Of value here is a critical understanding of labour markets and what influences the distribution of opportunities within them.

Career resilience involves the capability to cope with the ups and downs of working life. It is likely to be maintained through feelings of confidence and self-efficacy, hope, flexibility, self-esteem and self-reliance.

If we accept that this model covers most of the career issues that individuals need to deal with as their working lives progress, career counselling needs to attend to all three components. It should also be recognised though, as we argued earlier, that many presenting problems may not be all they seem, and they may reflect broader personal and emotional concerns.

Cultural Differences

Most of the theories discussed in this and previous chapters reflect European-American values of individualism, autonomy and the centrality of work in people's lives. Individuals from non-western cultures may not share these values, indeed research has identified certain values as being typical of particular cultural groups and nations.

Hofstede (2001), for example, in a study which first involved around 88,000 respondents employed by IBM in 72 countries, and was later supplemented by data from other populations unrelated to IBM, found five dimensions along which country cultures differ. These are as follows:

- Power distance – the extent to which less powerful employees and institutional members expect and accept that power is distributed unequally.
- Uncertainty avoidance – the extent to which a culture socialises its members to feel either uncomfortable or comfortable in unstructured situations.
- Individualism vs collectivism – how far individuals are expected to look after themselves or stay integrated within groups, for example around the family.
- Masculinity vs femininity – the ways in which emotional roles are distributed between the genders. Tough 'masculine' societies are contrasted with tender 'feminine' societies.
- Long-term vs short-term orientation – the extent to which a culture socialises its members to accept delayed gratification of their social, emotional and material needs.

Of these, the individualism–collectivism dimension is particularly relevant in understanding career development. The importance of social relationships in collectivist cultures suggests that career decisions will be strongly influenced by significant others, such as parents, partners and close friends. It has also been argued that once in employment, the main determinant of job satisfaction for those from collectivist cultures may be the extent to which the work role is approved by other people, not necessarily congruence between the individual's work values and values reinforced by the job (Brown, 2002). Other work suggests that the mechanisms underlying the pursuit of career success may differ between collectivist and individualist cultures. In the former, because personal failure reflects negatively on the group of which the individual is a member, it may be more important to avoid failure than to pursue success (Lehman, Chiu & Schaller, 2004).

In addition to values, other cultural differences are also likely to be important in the career development of individuals from different cultures. These include differences in time perspective, decision-making style (Leong & Hartung, 2000), ideas about reality, sense of morality, use of language and non-verbal behaviour, gender relations and the expression of emotion (McLeod, 2003). With regard to views of reality, for example, in western cultures people tend to have a *dualistic* view of reality, seeing the world as reflecting a mind–body split. Because of this western culture has developed various concepts that refer solely to mental phenomena, for example, guilt and anxiety. In cultures with more holistic views of mind, body and spirit, however, individuals are more likely to complain about physical ailments. Regarding language, some cultures find it difficult to talk about themselves in abstract terms and to tell stories in a linear way.

Therefore practitioners need to integrate multicultural perspectives into their understanding of career development and into their career counselling work. Somewhat optimistically, Leong and Hartung (2000) argue that with increasing multiculturalism in our societies, a 'multicultural mindset' is developing. As we have more social interaction with those from other cultures, our flexibility in relating to others increases. There are dangers though in assuming that we understand another's cultural background, not least because there is considerable diversity between the values systems of the same cultural groups. Practitioners should take care not to stereotype clients, perhaps adopting an attitude of cultural naïveté and curiosity, using 'cultural empathy' to explore with the client what their cultural background means to them (Ridley & Lingle, 1996).

Summary

The intention in this chapter was to provide an overview of adult development. First, stage theories were introduced, and these can be viewed as tools to think with in career counselling. Erikson's epigenetic theory focuses on ego development and is based on clinical work. Levinson's work is more empirically grounded and his idea of the Dream, the importance of mentor relationships, and the processes of reviewing, modifying the life-structure and individuation suggests that people can be helped, via the process of anticipatory socialisation, to look ahead to developmental tasks they may face in the future. We then discussed continuity and narrative theories of the life course. Career counsellors working within these orientations help individuals develop coherent stories about their lives and identify dominant themes.

Theories and models of adult career development which have implications for career counselling include Super's life-career rainbow, Nicholson's model of work-role transitions and Hall's model of psychological success. Models which view the life course in terms of periods of transition and learning suggest that career counsellors need to help individuals interpret their experiences in terms of 'mini-cycles' of transition as well as age-related stages and tasks. These kinds of approaches, along with other more interactive models of career development, emphasise the importance of on-going negotiations between individuals and employers. They also suggest that individuals need a range of career skills in the current context. These include decision-making skills, career management skills and career resilience.

The chapter concluded with a discussion of cultural differences in values, and career counsellors need to be aware that many theories of adult and career development reflect values which may not be held by those from non-Western cultures.

Discuss and Debate

1   Try to divide the lifespan into a series of stages. Where would you place the boundaries between the stages? Can you identify the main features of each stage, in terms of: (a) key tasks; (b) society's expectations; (c) the kinds of roles that are most common?

2   Give some thought to Levinson's early and middle adulthood stages and the accompanying tasks. How far did (or do) these stages and tasks seem to make sense in your own life? What are the implications for your career? How far do you think your experience of these stages and tasks is related to your gender or ethnic background?

3   What kind of psychological contract do you have with your employer? What do you offer, and what do you expect your organisation to provide? Are your expectations reciprocated? Has the psychological contract changed over time? Does this seem a useful way of describing your career?

4   How might you explain the finding that individuals who are 'on schedule' with regard to major family events are less likely to see career change as problematic as those who are 'off schedule'?

THREE   Counselling Theories

As we saw earlier, career and personal concerns are often so closely intertwined that it is unhelpful to see the practice of career counselling as somehow separate from therapeutic counselling. For example, clients can often become depressed or anxious and they will need support in dealing with these conditions. Helping clients manage their careers will therefore inevitably involve using skills and approaches derived from therapeutic counselling. In this chapter we examine some of the major perspectives on counselling and consider the implications of these for careers work. Four perspectives are discussed: person-centred, psychodynamic, cognitive-behavioural and narrative, and this is followed by a consideration of how different approaches can be combined.

Person-centred Theories

The person-centred approach to therapeutic counselling was first introduced by Rogers (1942). He used the term 'client-centred' to describe his orientation, implying that it is the client who tends to determine the focus of the counselling session. It has been one of the most commonly practised orientations to counselling and psychotherapy over the last half century.

The essence of the person-centred approach is that the most important influence on the progress made in the counselling session is the relationship between the counsellor and the client. Interview techniques are relatively unimportant; instead the attitudes and qualities of the counsellor are the main focus.

These attitudes and qualities are normally described as:

- Congruence (or genuineness) – being integrated and real in the relationship.
- Unconditional positive regard – respecting the client in a non-judgemental way.
- Empathic understanding – understanding the client from his or her own internal frame of reference, and trying to communicate this with the client.

Rogers (1957: 96) described the 'necessary and sufficient conditions of therapeutic personality change' as incorporating these qualities in the following way.

1   Two persons are in psychological contact.
2   The first, whom we shall term the client, is in a state of incongruence, being vulnerable and anxious.
3   The second person, whom we shall term the therapist, is congruent or integrated in the relationship.
4   The therapist experiences unconditional positive regard for the client.
5   The therapist experiences an empathic understanding of the client's internal frame of reference, and endeavours to communicate this to the client.
6   The communication to the client of the therapist's empathic understanding and unconditional positive regard is to a minimal degree achieved.

No other conditions are necessary. If these six conditions exist, and continue over a period of time, this is sufficient. The process of constructive personality change will follow.

It is worth at this point elaborating a little on Rogers' concepts of 'congruence', 'unconditional positive regard' and 'empathy'.

Congruence

Discussing congruence, Rogers states that the counsellor or therapist:

> ...should be, in the confines of this relationship, a congruent, genuine, integrated person...It is not necessary (nor is it possible) that the therapist be a paragon who exhibits this degree of integration, of wholeness, in every aspect of his life. It is sufficient that he is accurately himself [sic] in this hour of his relationship, that in this basic sense he is what he actually is, in this moment of time. (Rogers, 1957: 97)

Interestingly, Rogers includes being afraid of one's client or being aware of being distracted by one's own problems as examples of how the counsellor may be congruent, or genuine. Also, the counsellor's 'willingness to be known' is an important element of congruence (Barrett-Lennard, 1986). It is not so much a skill to be used, but a basic attitude.

McLeod (2003) identifies several effects that congruence has on the therapeutic process, including the point that if the counsellor accepts and expresses his or her own feelings of uncertainty and vulnerability it is easier for clients to accept their own; it helps to develop trust in the relationship; and it models one of the intended therapeutic outcomes.

Unconditional positive regard

According to Rogers, unconditional positive regard is demonstrated in the counselling relationship:

> To the extent that the therapist finds himself experiencing a warm acceptance of each aspect of the client's experience as being a part of that client, he is experiencing unconditional positive regard. (Rogers, 1957: 98)

In Rogers' view, helping clients accept their own experiences involves the counsellor accepting those experiences and feelings. This acceptance needs to be experienced genuinely by the therapist and communicated to the client. This can be achieved to some extent by using the technique of 'reflection' of the content of the client's statements and the feelings that lie behind them. But it may also entail the development of attitudes of acceptance by the counsellor. These attitudes may take longer to develop than learning the apparently straightforward technique of reflection. Rogers was, in fact, very critical about attempts to reduce person-centred counselling to a set of skills. He argued that the fundamental quality of the relationship and the attitude of the therapist need time to develop, and they cannot be emulated by a mechanical display of particular techniques (Rogers, 1957).

Unconditional positive regard relates closely to Rogers' ideas about 'conditions of worth'. He took the view that parents who frequently establish 'conditions of worth' for their children by giving them covert messages like 'I will only value or love you if...', are likely to interfere with the child's own process of self-valuation. He suggests that the counselling relationship should be free of 'conditions of worth' partly to provide a climate of acceptance in which the client's tendency to 'self-actualisation' can manifest itself.

Wilkins (2000) argues that of all the core conditions, unconditional positive regard is probably the most important, but it is the condition that presents the most challenge to counsellors. He suggests that we need to accept that our ability to offer unconditional positive regard is limited, but counsellors need to discover these limits and try to expand them.

Empathy

Empathy involves an understanding of the client's perceptions, experiences and feelings. However, this understanding does not mean that the therapist has the same or similar feelings. Rogers describes empathy as:

> To sense the client's private world as if it were your own, but without ever losing the 'as if' quality – this is empathy, and this seems essential for therapy. To sense the client's anger, fear, confusion as if it were your own, yet without your own anger, fear, or confusion getting bound up in it... . (Rogers, 1957: 99)

We should be clear about the distinction between empathy and sympathy. In contrast to empathy, sympathy often involves a seemingly supportive statement that does not necessarily address the client's experience. For example, the counsellor responses that are more likely to convey sympathy are: 'what a shame' or 'oh dear, well never mind'. Empathic responses, on the other hand, directly acknowledge the client's perspective, for example, 'you seem quite upset' or 'that sounds deeply distressing for you'.

Recent discussions of empathy have shifted the emphasis away from defining it as a trainable skill, towards a wider interpretation of it, as a component of an 'authentic commitment to be engaged in the world of the other' (McLeod, 2003).

Also, the client needs to *perceive* the counsellor as accepting and empathic for the counselling process to be effective. This is an important issue in both practice and research. In practice the counsellor needs to *communicate* empathy and acceptance, and the client needs to *experience* these qualities. In research, independent observers' ratings of counsellors on the empathy demonstrated may lack validity, since it is the client's experience of the counsellor's understanding that is crucial.

McLeod (2003), in his review of research carried out to assess the effectiveness of the person-centred approach, argues that the evidence suggests that Rogers was largely correct in his proposition that the conditions are not only necessary but also sufficient conditions for positive personality change.

Implications for career counselling

One of the first writers to explore how person-centred principles could be applied in career counselling was Patterson (1964). More recently, Bozarth and Fisher (1990) have elaborated further the key characteristics of a person-centred approach to career counselling. Their definition is as follows:

> Person-centered career counseling is a relationship between a counselor and a client, arising from the client's concerns, which creates a psychological climate in which the client can evolve a personal identity, decide the vocational goal that is fulfillment of that identity, determine a planned route to that goal, and implement that plan. The person-centered career counselor relates with genuineness, unconditional positive regard, and empathy; the locus of control for decisions remains with the client out of the counselor's trust in the self-actualizing tendency of the individual. The focus in person-centered career counseling is that of attitudes and beliefs that foster the natural actualizing process rather than on techniques and goals. (Bozarth & Fisher, 1990: 54)

Bozarth and Fisher argue that person-centred career counselling may remain strictly job focused, but it may well develop into other forms of counselling, including therapeutic counselling, depending on the client's needs. The issue of how far person-centred career counselling should incorporate the giving of career information has divided writers. Spokane (1991), for example, argues that all career counsellors should provide occupational information, and criticises person-centred theory for ignoring external constraints on decision making.

Bozarth and Fisher (1990), on the other hand, ask why any counselling theory should attend to occupational or labour market information more thoroughly than any other external variable that affects individuals in distress. They argue that it is only necessary that 'theory accurately conceptualises, and that the practitioner accurately understands, the client's need, addresses that need in counseling, and correctly guides the client to appropriate sources of information outside of the counseling setting' (Bozarth & Fisher, 1990: 112). Practitioners' stance on this issue will depend on the setting in which they work and their own preferences about their role. In the UK, practitioners working in the public sector will be expected to provide information, while those working independently will have more scope to define their own role.

Using a case study, Lent (1996) provides a useful illustration of some of the limitations of approaches which are directive, and 'nonperson-centred'. A 35-year-old single woman with high academic attainment approached a US college counselling service for help in choosing a health-related course. She was given interest and career maturity inventories and these showed that she had average scores on the Holland realistic, investigative and social occupational interests; a very high level of career decision-making ability; but little knowledge of health-related occupations. The case is discussed from a range of perspectives, including developmental and person-centred. Lent discusses how the developmental approach ignored the discrepancy between the client's presentation of her problem and what she said during the interview and assessment, probably because the developmental approach rarely addresses distorted perceptions or more subtle suggestions of emotional distress. The person-centred approach, on the other hand, identified some inconsistencies in the initial presentation of the problem and follow-up sessions were recommended to rule out a traumatic sexual experience. It turned out that the client had been raped, and this event had affected the woman's approach to her career. This had been missed by the other approaches.

Broadly, the person-centred approach emphasises attitudes and beliefs rather than techniques and goals. It is a phenomenological approach. Phenomenology takes the view that individuals react to events according to how they experience, perceive or interpret them, rather than to the events themselves. Also, the self-concept plays a key role in this approach. Super's (1963) propositions concerning the role of self-concepts in career development are frequently referred to.

The person-centred approach and
personal construct psychology

Surprisingly, few links have been made between the person-centred approach and personal construct psychology (PCP) (Kelly, 1955). PCP is a theory of personality which emphasises the unique ways in which people make sense of the world. Since it is essentially concerned with individuals' unique experiences, and with choice and change, one would expect that career counsellors with a person-centred orientation to their work would incorporate more ideas from PCP.

The main building block of PCP is the *construct*, which discriminates between objects of individuals' experiences. Constructs are *bi-polar*, that is they are described in terms of opposite ends of a dimension. For example, a construct an individual may use to describe jobs might be: well-paid – poorly-paid. PCP sees individuals as constantly testing out and elaborating their systems of constructs.

The PCP approach to career counselling sees the career counsellor as trying to understand how the client construes the world. Techniques used include:

- Eliciting constructs by asking clients to describe ways in which certain 'elements' (for example, jobs) are similar or different.
- 'Laddering' up the hierarchy of constructs from concrete subordinate constructs to superordinate constructs which have a broader application (one way of doing this is to probe *why* certain things are important to the individual).
- 'Pyramiding' down the hierarchy of constructs from superordinate constructs to subordinate ones (for example, by asking *how* things differ).
- Asking the client to complete a grid using particular constructs with a small range of elements (possibly jobs).
- Employing self-characterisation (for example, asking clients to describe how they see themselves in a particular position at work).
- Encouraging clients to develop action plans by moving towards tighter constructs.

One criticism that might be made of PCP as applied to career counselling is its lack of attention to objective reality. It is not clear, for example, how concrete data about work are incorporated into career counselling.

Psychodynamic Theories

Psychodynamic approaches to counselling are rooted in the work of Freud (see, for example Freud, 1933/1973). Since Freud's work and his method of treatment, psychoanalysis, became widely known, numerous writers and therapists have developed and modified his theories and ideas, and many counsellors work within the psychodynamic tradition, whilst not practising psychoanalysis as such.

The main features of the psychodynamic approach include: an assumption that individuals' difficulties have their origins in childhood experiences; the recognition that individuals may not be consciously aware of their motives; and the use in therapy or counselling of the interpretation of the transference relationship.

Levels of consciousness

Freud suggested that we have several levels of consciousness. Thoughts that we are aware of are said to be in the part of the *conscious* mind. In contrast, the *unconscious* is the part of mental life that is outside direct awareness. The *preconscious*, the third part of the mind, contains thoughts that could come into the conscious, although we are unaware of them.

Freud also viewed the mind as divided into three regions: the *id*, the *ego* and the *superego*. The id contains unconscious drives and impulses that make gratuitous demands for satisfaction. The ego is the largely conscious part of the mind that is most concerned with external reality. The superego develops through social interaction, mainly with parents, and represents the conscience. The restraining forces of the ego are often at odds with the demands of the id. Freud's model of personality is a dynamic one, with the ego struggling to deal with the conflicting demands of the id and the superego.

Defence mechanisms

An important activity in psychodynamic counselling is the identification and analysis of resistances and defences. Defence mechanisms tend to operate at an unconscious level and serve to protect the ego from threats of one sort or another. They can be functional, by reducing anxiety, but they can also be dysfunctional in that individuals are often unaware of how they are using defence mechanisms, and they cause them to experience reality in a distorted way.

Denial, where individuals are unable to acknowledge that a particular event has happened, is one example of a defence mechanism. In career counselling, psychodynamic counsellors may describe a person who is unwilling to accept that they have been made redundant, for example, as in denial. *Repression* is another example of a defence mechanism. This occurs when a threatening memory or perception becomes unavailable at a conscious level, and the individual therefore forgets events.

Projection as a defence mechanism involves seeing and exaggerating characteristics of oneself in others. These characteristics are often undesirable ones. For example, the behaviour of an individual who vehemently criticises someone else for acting in a certain way may be explained in these terms. Projection also forms the basis of some psychological assessment devices that involve presenting an ambiguous situation and inviting the individual to report their thoughts. Examples include sentence completion tests and the Rorschach ink blot test. Projective tests assume that individuals will respond to an ambiguous stimulus in a way that reveals aspects of their unconscious processes. *Introjection* is in a sense the converse of projection, in that characteristics perceived in others are seen as affecting the way individuals see themselves.

Displacement is said to occur when a strong negative emotion, for example anger, is not expressed directly to its source, but is displaced onto another person. For example, an interpretation of displacement may be made when a person who is angry with a superior is inhibited in expressing their anger, and then explodes with rage towards a more junior person for some trivial error. *Rationalisation* is an attempt to explain away some failure or shortcoming. *Reaction formation* describes the process where an individual has difficulty accepting a motive as their own and overcompensates by expressing an apparently opposite reaction. For example, in cases of prejudice, someone may appear to favour or criticise certain groups in a way that conceals their true motive. *Regression* is a label used by psychodynamic counsellors to describe behaviour which involves retreating into more child-like forms of behaviour when confronted with a difficult situation. Examples are speaking in a 'baby' voice, curling up and hugging oneself, or having temper tantrums.

The therapist–client relationship

Freud recognised that various phenomena occur in the interaction between therapist and patient. Some of these phenomena are desirable and helpful in the therapeutic process. Others, however, are less desirable, and could impede the process, and this is one reason why therapists working in this tradition are required to undergo their own therapy whilst working with clients.

Introjection can occur in therapists when, for example, they begin to experience emotions similar to those that their clients are experiencing. For example, a patient working with a depressed patient may begin to feel depressed themselves. *Resistance* is said to occur when a client moves away from material that could be distressing or threatening. *Transference* is a phenomenon that is said to occur when the client relates to the therapist as if they were an important figure in their life, for example, their father. Expressions of emotion, such as anger, may be apparently directed at the therapist whilst the client is talking about their father. In psychoanalysis, this is seen as a critical point in therapy: a stage to be welcomed and worked with, in order to help the client remember, understand and process some of their reactions to their father. *Counter-transference* is a similar process to transference, only here the therapist is reminded by their client of someone who is important to the therapist.

When this happens, the therapist may begin to respond to their client as if they were this other person. Counter-transference is seen as a source of interference in the therapy. Psychodynamic therapists are encouraged to identify this process quickly and deal with it in supervision sessions with their own therapist.

There is only space here for this very brief outline of some of the key concepts of the psychodynamic approach. The reader is referred to Freud (1933/1973), to McLeod (2003) and to M. Jacobs (1999), who provide useful general overviews of the approach.

Is psychodynamic theory valid?

The issue of how far psychodynamic theory represents a model of human nature which can be shown empirically to be valid has been debated for many years. To test its validity, it would be necessary to be able to describe the whole of the theory as a set of testable propositions. Unfortunately, however, many of the concepts within the theory are loosely defined, or defined merely by reference to other parts of the theory. Consequently, it is difficult to define the concepts in terms of observable events.

Some writers have claimed that because many aspects of psychodynamic theory cannot be proved empirically it has no value as a scientific approach within psychology (see, for example, Eysenck, 1972). On the other hand, it could be argued that its validity is based on making detailed observations of patients' experiences and behaviour in clinical settings. However, this is a dangerous approach to building theory. Freud's work was based mainly on his clinical work in Austria and many of his patients were mentally ill, and it is inappropriate to generalise from this sub-set of individuals to the whole of the human race.

But one might ask how far it is necessary that therapeutic approaches should be rooted in scientific acceptability. Perhaps if psychodynamic therapy is helpful to people the validity of Freudian theory is immaterial. We will discuss the effectiveness of therapy later, in Chapter 4.

Implications for career counselling

Career counsellors make less use of psychodynamic theories and concepts than theories and concepts derived from other models of individual development. Nevertheless, some concepts derived from psychodynamic theories can be helpful in informing thinking about career development. Watkins and Savickas (1990) have assessed the relevance of psychodynamic theory to career counselling and discussed some techniques and methods derived from this approach. For example, they argue that one advantage of psychodynamic career counselling is that it complements the objective perspective with the subjective. The objective view enables career counsellors to compare the client with other people (in terms of personality traits for example), and the subjective position enables them to understand clients' unique life themes. Integrating the objective and subjective pictures is helpful in enabling clients to relate their 'inner reality' to their 'outer reality'.

Watkins and Savickas (1990) suggest that four types of clients appear to benefit greatly from a psychodynamic approach. The first type are those who are indecisive, unrealistic or naïve. The second are those who are 'difficult' cases. A psychodynamic perspective often reveals misconceptions, leaving them more free to develop their careers. The third type are adults who already have an objective view of their interests and abilities. Lastly, there is a group of clients who may be 'culturally different' and therefore may not be well served by an objective view that draws on views of reality that are different from their own.

One common aim of psychodynamic career counselling is to identify 'life themes', and career counsellors need to develop the skill of sensing patterns in people's lives in order to assess these themes. Structured interviews and projective techniques may be used in career assessment to identify themes, and an example of an interview technique is discussed in Chapter 6. However, it is debatable whether counsellors need to adhere to a psychodynamic approach to develop skill in identifying life themes. Many career counsellors take an eclectic approach to their work, drawing on diverse perspectives and techniques. We will discuss theoretical diversity in more depth later in this chapter.

Person-centred and psychodynamic approaches compared

At this point, it may be useful to consider some similarities and differences between the two approaches to therapeutic counselling we have discussed so far: person-centred and psychodynamic. In terms of models of psychological development, person-centred approaches take a phenomenological perspective, which is relatively unconcerned with the content of past experience. Yet they recognise the importance in childhood of unconditional acceptance by parents. The emphasis is mainly on self-awareness and self-evaluation, and the idea of 'congruence' in development is important. In contrast, psychodynamic approaches often focus on the content of past experience, particularly in early childhood. There is an emphasis too on psychosexual development. The idea of psychic conflict has some similarities to the person-centred notion of incongruence.

With regard to techniques used by the counsellors and therapists adhering to the two approaches, in person-centred counselling the aim is to facilitate insight in order to produce change, and the emphasis is on the egalitarian quality of the relationship between the client and the therapist. Therapist self-disclosure is encouraged. Also, any interpretations that are made are based on the client's specific experiences. Psychodynamic counsellors also emphasise the quality of the relationship between the client and the practitioner, but this is less egalitarian, and the roles of each party are strictly interpreted. Facilitating client insight is essential too, but this uses psychodynamic concepts. Therapist self-disclosure is less important. There is more emphasis on defence mechanisms and transference processes, and interpretations go beyond what is conscious to the client.

Owen (1999) has written at some length about the similarities and differences between the two types of therapy. In particular, he argues that both approaches rely on the communication of empathy. The psychodynamic literature analyses this process in terms of defences against anxiety and unpleasant feelings. The person-centred approach, on the other hand, is more concerned with how therapists can develop and communicate empathy to their clients. It is interesting that Rogers' later writing draws on ideas about unconscious processes. He described his most intuitive moments thus:

> ...I am perhaps in a slightly altered state of consciousness.... My conscious intellect takes over. I [nonconsciously] know much more than my conscious mind is aware of. I do not form my responses consciously, they simply arise in me, from my nonconscious sensing of the world of the other. (Rogers (1986), quoted in Owen, 1999: 174)

Owen sees empathy as projection, in psychodynamic terms. It is a 'sense generated from within oneself that is given to the other person' (Owen, 1999: 174). He argues that rather than showing an enforced positive attitude towards clients, therapists should note their own negative and positive reactions to clients and use counter-transference in a helpful and respectful manner.

Cognitive-Behavioural Theories

In contrast to person-centred and psychodynamic approaches to counselling, which focus on self exploration and understanding, cognitive-behavioural approaches are less concerned with helping clients gain insight into their problems and more concerned with client action that will result in change. Cognitive-behavioural theories have their origins in behavioural psychology. They have three key features: a change-focused, problem-solving approach to work with clients; a concern with scientific values; and attention to the cognitive (thought) processes through which people monitor their behaviour.

Behavioural psychology is viewed as having been developed by Watson (1919). Watson was critical of introspection, a commonly used method of psychological research at the time, and argued that psychology should be concerned only with observable phenomena. It should therefore study actual, overt behaviour rather than thoughts, since it was only behaviour that could be controlled and measured in laboratory settings.

Later behaviourists, such as Skinner, drew on Watson's ideas to discover the laws of learning. They took the view that all the habits and beliefs exhibited by individuals must be learned, and therefore the most important objective for psychology was to find out how people learn. They also argued that the basic principles of learning would be similar in any organism, and so carried out their research predominantly on animals, rather than human beings.

The theories of learning developed by these early behaviourists (operant and classical conditioning) led to the application of behaviourist principles to the treatment of psychological problems. However, writers soon began to question the efficacy of therapy that relied exclusively on behaviourist ideas. Many behaviourist techniques rely on the capacity of clients to process information, and it was argued that therapy needed to take account of how clients thought about themselves. Around the same time, some psychodynamically oriented therapists began to take an interest in clients' thought processes. Beck (1976), for example, identified several different kinds of 'cognitive distortion' that needed to be addressed in counselling. One example is *over-generalisation*, where general conclusions are drawn about the self, or someone else, from very limited evidence. Another is *personalisation*, which involves a tendency to imagine that events are always attributable to one's actions.

Cognitive behavioural approaches take the view that how people react to events is largely determined by their views of them, not by the events themselves (Ellis, 1994). By examining and re-evaluating unhelpful thoughts individuals can develop and experiment with alternative viewpoints and behaviours that may be more effective. Scott and Dryden (2003) categorise the various cognitive behavioural approaches as those involving:

- Coping skills
- Problem solving
- Cognitive restructuring
- Structural cognitive therapy

Approaches that address coping skills may involve teaching clients what to say to themselves and how to respond in situations that they find difficult. Those that focus on problem solving involve the logical steps of defining the problem, generating as many alternative solutions as possible, and choosing and planning the best solution. Two therapies that deal with cognitive restructuring are rational emotive behaviour therapy and cognitive therapy. Both help clients revise inappropriate beliefs and interpretations of situations. Structural cognitive therapy takes a similar approach, but is more concerned with addressing core beliefs that developed early in life.

Whatever approach is taken, therapy begins with a well-planned rationale. Also, all the approaches provide training in skills that clients can use to increase their effectiveness in their daily lives, and they encourage them to attribute improvements to their own increased skilfulness rather than to therapists' interventions.

Implications for career counselling

Although few approaches to career counselling draw explicitly on cognitive-behavioural approaches, career and life coaching often incorporate these perspectives (e.g. Grant & Greene, 2001). Both Krumboltz's model (Mitchell & Krumboltz, 1996) and social cognitive career theory (discussed in Chapter 2) employ some cognitive-behavioural principles. Krumboltz's approach, derived from social learning theory (Bandura, 1977) suggests that people acquire beliefs about themselves and work through two kinds of learning experiences: instrumental and associative. Through instrumental learning individuals develop preferences for particular activities through their experiences of success which are rewarded. Associative learning occurs vicariously when individuals observe significant others being rewarded and punished for their behaviour. As consequences of these learning experiences, self-observation generalisations are made (beliefs about one's own abilities, interests, values, etc.), and task-approach skills are learned (for example, decision-making skills and orientations towards work). Over time, sequences of learning experiences enable individuals to develop self-observation generalisations and task-approach skills that form the basis for career development.

The tasks of the career counsellor working within this orientation are similar to those of the therapeutic counsellor. One important objective is to assess the 'accuracy, completeness and coherence' of clients' beliefs about themselves and the external world (Mitchell & Krumboltz, 1996).

The problems that inaccurate beliefs can produce include:

- Making inaccurate generalisations about work from one single experience
- Making social comparisons with an idealised role model
- Emotionally over-reacting to negative events
- Making invalid attributions of the causes of particular work-related events
- Self-deception

According to social learning theory, it is the career counsellor's role to challenge and counter these beliefs, by, for example, examining the assumptions underlying them, identifying inconsistencies and confronting illogical systems of beliefs. Furthermore, rational behaviour should be reinforced. Krumboltz's (1988) Career Beliefs Inventory can be used as a tool to identify attitudes and beliefs that are dysfunctional.

The techniques used by career counsellors in the cognitive-behaviourist tradition include:

- Modelling – where clients are exposed to live, taped or filmed models to demonstrate desired behaviour, for example seeking information.
- Behavioural rehearsal – where appropriate behaviours in certain areas where clients are having difficulty are defined, and they are encouraged to role play the desired behaviours and try them out in real life. For example, assertiveness training can be done in this way.

Narrative Approaches

It has been argued that we are now in a 'postmodern' era, where over-arching theories or systems of thought such as Marxism or psycho-analysis have lost their attraction. McLeod (2003) suggests that narrative approaches to counselling are in line with this shift to more local truths and knowledge systems.

As we saw in Chapter 2, writers and practitioners taking a narrative approach focus on the stories that clients tell about their lives, helping them make sense of their experiences and identify key themes. Rather than trying to verify objectively whether experiences and events described by clients actually occurred, the aim generally is to help clients understand and explain their experiences in a coherent way and retell or 're-author' their story or stories in a more satisfactory and 'agentic' manner. The approach is not entirely novel, however: many common 'taken-for-granted' counsellor interventions are consistent with a narrative approach. Empathic reflection, for example, can help clients find and tell their stories, and the skill of challenging can be used to draw clients' attention to inconsistencies and contradictions in their narratives.

The term 'narrative therapy' covers a range of perspectives and techniques. Luborsky and Crits-Christoph (1990), for example, take the view that the stories told by clients convey information about individuals' habitual ways of relating to other people. Consistent themes and conflicts run through these stories, and these are called core conflictual relationship themes. It is also suggested that these stories are structured around three elements: the wish of the individual in relation to others; the response of the other person; and the response of the self. Overall, the most frequently reported client wishes are 'to be close and accepted', 'to be loved and understood' and 'to assert self and be independent'. The most common responses from other people are 'rejecting and opposing' and 'controlling', and the most common responses of the self are 'disappointed and depressed', 'unreceptive' and 'helpless' (Luborsky, Popp, Luborsky & Mark, 1994). Luborsky and Crits-Christoph (1990) argue that interpretations based on this model are helpful in providing insight into clients' problems.

Another way of using narrative approaches in therapeutic counselling is through the use of constructivist techniques, such as metaphors. Constructivist counselling focuses on the ways people give meaning to their lives, and metaphors may help the client describe a difficult event by helping them describe what the event was like. For example, the grief of bereavement may be likened to a physical wound: one cannot force it to heal, and neither can one force a psychological wound to heal. Gonclaves (1995) is one therapist who uses metaphors, training clients in methods of generating metaphoric associations to their life stories, and helping them construct alternative metaphors which help them develop more of a sense of 'authorship' in their lives.

Another approach to narrative counselling has developed out of a social constructionist orientation. Social constructionism sees experience as shaped by the social environment, and it questions whether an inner psychological reality exists. From this perspective, narrative is a bridge between individual experience and the cultural system. According to White and Epston (1990), one of the key features of narrative therapy is helping the client externalise the problem.

As Lock, Epston, Maisel and de Faria (2005: 321) argue, 'the person is not the problem, the problem is the problem'. Moreover, separating the person and the problem reveals that the problem is actually the person's relationship with the problem. A person with anorexia, for example, can be helped by being encouraged to stop identifying themselves as 'an anorexic', and to separate themselves from their condition, inspecting and challenging its hold on them.

Other work uses the notion of 'discursive positioning', a term introduced by Davies and Harre (1990), which builds on Foucault's concept of 'subjective positioning'. In conversation, individuals attempt to establish positions for themselves both in relation to the person to whom they are speaking, and in relation to social discourse (language and meanings) in general. A counselling session can therefore be viewed as an opportunity to develop an alternative position within a discourse. Winslade (2005: 358) suggests that a session might proceed through the following steps:

1 Build trust in a relationship and explore the problem(s) that brings a person to counselling.
2 Develop an externalising conversation that deconstructs the problem story and locates it in the world of discourse.
3 Map the discursive positions that the person is invited into by the problem story.
4 Identify the person's efforts to resist being positioned in this way.
5 Inquire into the person's preferences for the kind of re-positioning that would make a difference.
6 Develop an account of such position changes that is located in personal history, in a community of membership and also in alternative discourses/knowledges that can serve to sustain the positioning shift in the face of the continued assertion of dominant discourses.

One of Winslade's (2005) examples of fictitious counselling exchanges shows how Rhonda, an African-American woman, has been struggling to resist the dominant discursive positions based on race and gender that she is offered by family members. The counsellor attempts to give her the space to reposition herself in relation to this discourse.

Rhonda: My family say things to me like, why are you wanting to go and study more? Why don't you get a proper job? Why don't you find yourself a man and get married?

Counsellor: So do these messages get to you, do they get under your skin?

Rhonda: Yeah they make it hard. But they don't stop me. I have had to work hard on myself not to believe that stuff, not to give in to those values. Sometimes I have to give myself a poke and say, look around you. Look at what they are wanting for you. Is that enough to make life worth living? It's hard but I keep thinking, who wants to be satisfied with a life that's not worth much?

Counsellor: So does it feel like those family stories are betraying you through not supporting your hopes and dreams?

Rhonda: Yeah well a bit. But it's not them really, that's society speaking. Think about it. We women learn that if you don't have a man, if you don't have a relationship, you're nothing. So we go out of our way for a relationship. Even if we know that this man is not treating us right, even if he is cheating on us, we will go out of our way to make it work. Why? Because we don't want to be thought of as less than…So we put up with a lot of things that we shouldn't have to. That's why it's important to me to get myself together now so that my children in future see something different. (Winslade, 2005: 360–1)

Implications for career counselling

Several writers on career counselling have written persuasively about the power of career narratives. Cochran (1997), for example, argues that career counselling is distinguished from other forms of counselling by focusing particularly on narratives that deal with future career development. He also emphasises the importance of helping clients 'actualise an ideal narrative', achieving what they would ideally like to do. This involves:

- Wholeness, or a coherent story
- Harmony among values and activities
- Sense of agency, or being proactive and responsible for one's actions
- Fruitfulness, or a sense of progress in dealing with career challenges

Simon and Osipow's (1996) term 'vocational script' is broadly similar to Cochran's idea of the 'career narrative'. A vocational script is 'a person's unique characterization of vocational identity independent of specific jobs, positions, and careers' (1996: 153). For example, one may describe oneself as having a clear sense of direction, as a good leader and the producer of novel ideas. These kinds of descriptions are often overlooked when older workers describe their careers, for example, many see themselves as 'plateauing', and see their usefulness declining.

Simon and Osipow identify three types of intervention which help clients develop their narrative. The first is engaging in a *life review*. Clients are asked to write down a series of key events. This includes events connected to relationships, and failures and successes more generally. Next, clients allocate levels of importance to each event according to the amount of autonomy and agency they experienced at the time. This enables clients to engage in the activities of 'delineation, definition, values clarification, and synthesis' (Simon & Osipow, 1996: 159).

Secondly, clients are helped to *define their work experience as a career*, identifying patterns of preferences and skills, rewards sought and gained, and behavioural responses. The vocational script can then begin to take shape, providing a link between work and non-work activities. Lastly, the individual is helped to *apply the vocational script to career planning*. As part of this process, the 'career definition becomes a story of the self persevering, building autonomy and personal agency, feeling productive, and bringing these patterns into the future' (Simon & Osipow, 1996: 160).

Another promoter of the narrative approach is Savickas. In one of his latest writings (Savickas, 2005) he presents an instructive example of a 'Career Style Interview', which includes questions about clients' role models, favourite books and TV programmes, leisure activities and favourite sayings. Clients' early recollections are also asked for, and they are asked to give each recollection a headline or title. The counsellor's interpretation includes identifying verbs in early recollections (for example, if 'talking' appears, this suggests that the client likes to communicate). The headlines composed for the recollections are then examined: these are seen as 'rhetorical compressions' describing the gist of the story. For instance, one client's headline for a story about how she was told not to move around in a camper van while on a trip with her grandparents and uncle was 'Little girl annoyed because she must sit still'. This was seen as indicating how powerful individuals stopped her pursuing her dreams, and also that she wanted her counsellor to encourage her to move on in her career development and help her speak up for herself.

Law's (1996) work on 'career learning' also takes what amounts to a narrative perspective on career counselling. He argues that career support is not simply concerned with identifying the individual's inherent aptitudes and interests and matching them to opportunities. It is rather a process which engenders possibilities for individuals by engaging them in educative processes. Career counselling is therefore essentially *educative*, helping individuals learn, sift and make sense of material in order to come to a greater understanding of themselves.

Narrative approaches to career counselling seem to accord with Bruner's (2002) view that 'self is a perpetually rewritten story', and we are defined and constituted by our narratives of ourselves. We create the self by 'writing' and 'storying' it, and with help these narratives can become more coherent and meaningful.

But are we continuously constructing a story out of our lives, and if we are not, ought we to be? And how much does it matter that narrative approaches to counselling cannot establish the truth of the facts underlying a narrative? It is likely that telling and retelling past experiences leads to changes and embellishments, and it may be that the more one retells one's story, the further one moves away from self-knowledge (Strawson, 2004).

Epistemological issues

Contrasting narrative approaches with the orientations discussed at the beginning of this chapter and in earlier chapters highlights important epistemological issues (matters concerning the nature of knowledge). For several decades, career theory and counselling theory have been dominated by liberal-humanism. The self has been viewed as a stable, independent entity which can be best understood using objective methods, and the individual's capacity for choice and autonomy has been emphasised. The interest in narrative approaches to career counselling is an example of the broader enthusiasm for postmodern ideas which examine the 'wider socio-cultural fabric in which we are all intertwined' (Sinclair & Monk, 2005) and the discourses which inform social life. From this Foucaultian perspective, language and discourse affect how we understand ourselves and how counsellors work with their clients. Rather than display (relatively) static traits, for example abilities and interests, individuals are seen as speaking and acting in relation to particular contexts and to the discourses they have taken up. People experience multiple and competing discourses at any one time, and so any 'objective understanding' of the self is impossible.

Comparing and Integrating Theories

So far in this chapter, we have discussed four approaches to therapeutic counselling and looked at some of their implications for career counselling. Table 3.1 summarises some of the main strengths and weaknesses of these approaches.

Eclecticism and integration

Over the years there have been several attempts to combine two or more approaches to counselling to form a hybrid, eclectic or integrative approach. Many of the approaches discussed so far have been influenced by earlier work and sometimes the differences between them are mainly ones of emphasis.

Ivey was one of the first writers to move away from theoretical dogma to focus on the skills and practices used by counsellors (see, for

Table 3.1 Strengths and weaknesses of four approaches to career counselling

Approach	Strengths	Weaknesses
Person-centred	Rogers' ideas have influenced a wide range of therapeutic practices, not only person-centred counselling	The core conditions are unlikely to be sufficient in career counselling, where information is frequently needed
Psychodynamic	Provides a sophisticated conceptual framework from which to view the client's development; the theory is still developing	Many propositions are difficult to test empirically
Cognitive-behavioural	Suggests straightforward practical techniques which lend themselves well to evaluations of effectiveness	Pays little attention to the relationship between the career counsellor and the client
Narrative	Since we all tell 'stories' in everyday life about our experiences, it makes sense to use these in career counselling	Different interpretations of narrative approaches could lead to confusion

example, Ivey & Authior, 1978). He emphasised the importance of a range of skills in counselling, including attending behaviour (e.g. appropriate eye contact and body language), and reflection of meaning, reflection of feeling, skills of structuring the interview, and confrontation. Egan (2002), in his 'skilled helper' model, also focused on skills, within a stage model of counselling. His is a problem management approach involving the following stages (Egan, 2002: 21):

Stage I: 'What's Going On?' Helping Clients Clarify the Key Issues Calling for Change
The Three Steps of Stage I
Step I-A: Help clients tell their *stories*
Step I-B: Help clients break through *blind spots* that prevent them from seeing themselves, their problem situations, and their unexplored opportunities as they really are
Step I-C: Help clients choose the *right* problems and/or opportunities to work on

Stage II: 'What Solutions Make Sense for Me?' Helping Clients Determine Outcomes
The Three Steps of Stage II
Step II-A: Help clients use their imaginations to spell out *possibilities for a better future*
Step II-B: Help clients choose *realistic and challenging goals* that are real solutions to the key problems and unexplored opportunities identified in Stage I

Step II-C: Help clients find the *incentives* that will help them *commit* themselves to their change agendas

Stage III: 'What Do I Have to Do to Get What I Need or Want?' Helping Clients Develop Strategies for Accomplishing Goals
The Three Steps of Stage III
Step III-A: Possible Actions: Help clients see that there are many different ways of achieving goals
Step III-B: Help clients choose best-fit strategies
Step III-C: Help clients craft a plan

Action: 'How Do I Get Results?' Helping Clients Implement Their Plans

The Egan model can be viewed as a 'map' by which the usefulness of elements from other approaches can be located and assessed. For example, empathy (a concept taken from person-centred therapy) is seen as a key communication skill throughout the process.

Some writers (e.g. Strupp, 1973) take the view that the commonalities within different forms of therapy are far greater than their differences. One way of identifying common theoretical principles, or common factors, is to focus on an intermediate level of abstraction, lying between theory and techniques. An example is developing and maintaining the therapeutic alliance.

Other attempts to combine theories of counselling and psychotherapy have been described as 'technical eclecticism' and 'theoretical integration' (Norcross & Grencavage, 1989). Technical eclecticism uses methods and techniques drawn from different sources, without necessarily adhering to their parent theories. Theoretical integration involves attempts to synthesise conceptually diverse frameworks.

In the late 1980s Norcross and Thomas conducted a survey to identify what was preventing more integration of approaches (Norcross & Thomas, 1988). Fifty-eight prominent integrationists rated, in terms of severity, twelve potential obstacles to integration. The most highly rated obstacle was 'intrinsic investment of individuals in their private perceptions and theories'. This took the form of 'egocentric, self-centered colleagues'; 'the institutionalisation of schools'; and 'ideological warfare, and factional rivalry'. The second most highly rated was 'inadequate training in more than one psychotherapy system'. The key training question is how to facilitate adequate knowledge and competence in the various orientations.

The third-ranked obstacle was 'approaches have divergent assumptions about psychopathology and health'. This concerns ontological and epistemological issues. Different orientations often have contradictory assumptions about human nature, the determinants of personality development, and the origins of psychopathology.

The fourth most highly rated obstacle was 'inadequate empirical research on the integration of psychotherapies'. Because of the dearth of research, practice tends not to be evidence based. Fifth in rank was 'absence of a "common" language for psychotherapists'. Each therapeutic orientation has its own jargon which widens the gulf between different approaches.

Since this study, however, there has been growing interest in and proliferation of integrative therapies. What is seen as integrationist today may be the single-school approach of tomorrow.

So what are the implications of these possible ways of combining approaches for career counsellors? Kidd (1996: 204) suggests that there is a range of options open to practitioners.

1 Stay with one or two models (if so, which and why?)
2 Identify the common features from various models that seem to produce client gains – the common factors approach.
3 Tease out the specific methods and techniques from the various models that produce client gains – technical eclecticism.
4 Try to come up with their own, unique, integrative model – theoretical integration.

However, it may be more important that career counsellors appreciate that it is possible to learn from the models that exist in a number of different ways. This may mean that tacit relationships between theories and techniques become more explicit. We can illustrate how this might work by examining the last two options: technical eclecticism and theoretical integration.

Technical eclecticism in career counselling

This approach assumes that it is not necessary to synthesise divergent models in order to use the techniques they suggest. As we have seen, different approaches to career counselling emphasise a range of different activities. Each of these is seen to contribute in some way to an effective intervention. However, it is difficult to select appropriate techniques without reference to specific criteria of effective career counselling. Some of these criteria are as follows.

Research into careers advisers' perceptions of effective interviewing (Kidd, Killeen, Jarvis & Offer, 1993) suggests that interviews are seen to be most effective when the careers adviser is able to clarify clients' expectations at the start of the interview (this may include drawing up a 'contract'), establish rapport with the client, challenge them to test their ideas against reality and structure the interview. We might also add two other criteria to this list, derived from the key issues identified by Taylor (1985) and Nathan and Hill (2006). These are: appropriate provision of information about opportunities and the recognition of the interdependence of personal and occupational concerns. A final criterion is suggested by

Holland, Magoon and Spokane's (1981) recognition that one of the main tasks of career counselling is to provide cognitive structures to help clients organise their thinking about self and situation. These features of effective interviewing involve the following activities.

- Clarifying expectations (or negotiating a 'contract') – agreeing the objectives for the interview and the nature of the guidance process. The latter includes making the responsibilities of the career counsellor and the client explicit.
- Developing rapport – using relationship skills, as well as more specific skills such as listening and reflecting.
- Effective challenging – helping clients to 'reality-test' their ideas about themselves and opportunities. This may include challenging unrealistic ideas or plans, gender stereotyping, inconsistent beliefs, mismatches of job ideas with local opportunities or abilities, and strategically unsound plans.
- Structuring the interview – having a clear sense of structure and being able to progress back and forth through interview stages in an interactive manner. This includes setting aside time at the end for action planning.
- Providing information appropriately – helping clients to relate information to themselves, discuss their feelings about information and evaluate the information. This includes encouraging clients to find sources of information for themselves.
- Recognising the interdependence of personal and occupational concerns – accepting that discussing career issues may involve sensitive personal issues and helping clients to deal with these. This includes recognising the boundaries between career counselling and personal counselling, and clarifying these for clients.
- Providing cognitive structures – helping clients to develop a conceptual framework within which to organise their ideas, so as to increase the breadth and depth of their thinking about self and situation.

Theoretical integration in career counselling

Over the last century, career counselling has progressed through a series of stages which reflect different views of careers (Kidd & Killeen, 1992). Initially, its aim was to make recommendations about job choices. Then from the 1960s, it began to be viewed as a facilitative activity, helping clients develop the autonomy to make informed choices in a wise manner. More recently, it has become more concerned with helping people develop the skills for lifelong career management, so that they are able to navigate their way in a changing labour market.

Different orientations to career counselling reflect these various purposes. Holland's work, for example, focused on choice of occupation, while person-centred approaches are more in line with facilitating the skills for lifelong career management.

Career counsellors need to be aware of these differences in ideologies, so that they may be able to judge how far each approach suits their own purposes in meeting the needs of different clients in a range of contexts. Arguably, career counsellors need to be helped to develop their own style, which moves beyond a technical combination of methods, through the process of theoretical integration. However, the situations in which career counselling is practised are often ambiguous and complex, and the intellectual effort in which practitioners engage to integrate knowledge and experience needs to be fairly sophisticated. Any model of practice which simply applies theoretical knowledge in a mechanistic and unproblematic way, therefore, is likely to be inadequate. Schon (1983) referred to this mechanistic approach as a 'technical rationality' model of practice. Within this model the role of academic knowledge is seen as superior to practitioners' 'coal face' experience and problem-solving skills.

One alternative model for professional learning is Schon's (1983) process of 'reflection-in-action'. Reflection is seen by Schon as the process through which practitioners come to recognise and integrate the knowledge they have gained through impressions and experience, as well as formal learning. Through this knowledge they are able to identify appropriate action. Thinking and acting are seen as being in a dynamic relationship, where attempts to understand a situation through action leads to changes in the situation, which in turn lead to new understandings and revised actions. This idea of the 'reflective practitioner' has become popular with some writers on career counselling and with some providers of training in career support. Collin (1996), for example, argues that an over-reliance on a positivist, technical-rational approach to training is unhelpful, given the complex practical settings within which practitioners operate. Instead, practitioners should become 'map-makers', using localised and contextualised knowledge to suit their purposes.

This suggests that the practitioner should be an active generator of new knowledge, improvising, adapting and elaborating existing theory, rather than simply applying it. This of course moves the focus on to the nature and rigour of the process through which the practitioner explores the situation and reflects on it, and away from the scientific rigour involved in the production of academic knowledge. This kind of exploration is challenging and can also be threatening, and this highlights the need for regular supervision for career counsellors. We discuss this in Chapter 9.

Emphasising the importance of the practitioner's own knowledge and reflection on experience has its dangers too. In particular, there is the possibility that useful concepts and models, developed through years of research, are ignored, in favour of anecdotes which are inevitably biased by the subjectivity of the practitioner. Reflective practice needs to include critical analysis of academic theory and research, as well as critical interpretation of the career counsellor's own experience. Training therefore should cover academic theory and research, encourage the development of skills of critical analysis of this work, and in addition set the trainee on a long-term path of professional development which has a self-reflective process at its heart.

Summary

Four orientations to therapeutic counselling were outlined in this chapter: person-centred theories; psychodynamic theories; cognitive-behavioural theories; and narrative approaches, together with eclectic and integrative approaches. Each of these has led to a particular orientation to career counselling. Person-centred approaches, such as that of Rogers, view the relationship between the client and the counsellor as the most important determinant of effective career counselling. The three key attitudes and qualities displayed by the counsellor are; congruence, unconditional positive regard and empathy. Facilitating 'self-actualisation' in clients is emphasised, as well as understanding their subjective reactions to events. Psychodynamic theories, which originated from the work of Freud, focus on early childhood experiences, defence mechanisms and transference processes. Psychodynamic career counsellors use these concepts in their work, and identifying life themes is also a common focus.

Cognitive-behavioural theories play down the importance of helping individuals gain insight into the matters that concern them, and instead are more concerned with action that will lead to change. Clients' cognitive processes are important, as is determining the accuracy and realism of their beliefs about their situation. A recent development is the narrative approach to counselling; this covers a range of perspectives. The terms 'vocational script' and 'career narrative' are used to describe the individual's career identity, developed through their life story.

Rather than adhere to one specific approach, many therapeutic and career counsellors prefer to combine approaches in one of three ways: the common factors approach; technical eclecticism; and theoretical integration. Each has its advantages and disadvantages.

Discuss and Debate

1 Are Rogers' 'necessary and sufficient conditions' indeed necessary and sufficient? What other qualities, skills or behaviours are needed in therapeutic counselling?
2 What are the similarities and differences between person-centred and psychodynamic counselling in terms of: (a) their model of psychological development; and (b) the techniques used?
3 Which of Mitchell and Krumboltz's guidelines for determining problematic beliefs and generalisations do you think are most useful? Why?
4 Think about the stories you tell about yourself when you describe your career to other people. How might you analyse these using a narrative approach?
5 Do you think that combining approaches to career counselling is a good way forward? What are the main obstacles to combining approaches?

FOUR Evaluating the Effectiveness of Career Counselling

So far in this volume we have discussed a range of approaches to career counselling. We turn now to consider the evidence for the effectiveness of career counselling and the methods by which it has been evaluated. We have argued that career counselling should be informed by therapeutic counselling practices. Accordingly, in our consideration of effectiveness it will be appropriate to include a discussion of the evaluation of therapeutic counselling, as well as career counselling.

The concept of *evidence-based practice* is increasingly used in discussions of the effectiveness of therapeutic counselling and psychotherapy. Evidence-based practice is best thought of as a process, rather than a one-off assessment of whether a particular intervention is effective. In essence, it requires practice to be based on evidence that it is effective, rather than relying on practitioners' preferences for one approach or technique or another. Baker and Kleijnen (2000) suggest that the process can be conceived as involving five stages:

1 The formulation of questions about effectiveness in such a way that they can be answered.
2 A search for the best evidence.
3 Assessment of that evidence for its validity and importance.
4 Application of approaches and techniques in practice.
5 Evaluation of effectiveness.

This chapter focuses on the research evidence relating to stage five, but it is important to recognise that useful research evidence depends very much on formulating appropriate research questions in the first place, as stage one suggests.

There is a distinction to be made between process research and outcome research. In process studies the researcher attempts to assess the therapeutic elements that are associated with change in the client. In contrast, outcome studies aim to discover how far a particular intervention has helped the client. Differences in the client before and after the intervention are examined, without identifying what actually happens within the counselling sessions.

Process Research

Process research into therapeutic counselling

An important focus in process research is the study of helping skills in therapeutic counselling. One methodology involves an experimental approach, where researchers manipulate a helping skill and observe the effects on an outcome variable. The advantage of using the experimental method is that skills can be clearly defined and other variables can be controlled. This gives the researcher more confidence that the manipulated (independent) variable led to the effects on the outcome variable. To the extent to which the independent variable is capable of affecting the outcome the experiment is said to have high internal validity. One disadvantage of this method is that the setting for the experiment is artificial, so the findings cannot be generalised to counselling taking place in a natural setting. This means that the study would have low external validity. Tepper and Haase (2001), for example, asked therapists and clients to watch videotapes in which therapists assumed different verbal and non-verbal stances, and to evaluate the therapists' levels of empathy, respect and genuineness. Differences in the ratings were assumed to be due to differences in verbal and non-verbal behaviours, because other factors were controlled.

Correlational methods are also used in process research. The frequency of occurrence of one process variable is related to another process variable, or to an outcome of therapy. For example, Fretz (2001) correlated the frequency of certain non-verbal behaviours with clients' perceptions of the therapist's respect for the client. Interestingly, the best indicator of respect was clasping the client's hand.

One advantage of the correlational approach is that it enables researchers to study naturally occurring events. One criticism, however, is that it fails to take account of the appropriateness of the process variable, or its timing. Discussing the example of frequency of counsellor interpretation as a process variable, Hill (2001) points out that one moderately deep interpretation of why a client is behaving in a certain way may be more helpful than ten badly timed interpretations. Also, one cannot draw any conclusions about cause and effect from any significant correlations. So, in the above example, one cannot necessarily conclude that hand clasping led to clients feeling respected. Instead, the relationship between the two variables – hand clasping and respect – could have been due to their both being correlated with another variable. For example, taking hold of the client's hand may reflect the therapist's need to communicate warmth, and it may be this that leads to clients feeling respected.

Other methodological approaches used in process research are sequential analyses and analyses of patterns. Sequential analyses involve the study of the immediate impact of one process variable on another. Hill, Helms, Tichenor, Spiegel, O'Grady and Perry (2001), for example, investigated links between the helping skills of the therapist and clients' insight into their difficulties. The highest levels of insight followed therapist self-disclosure, and the lowest followed direct guidance and confrontation. One problem with this method, however, is that it cannot take account of effects of interventions which are delayed over time. Analyses of patterns is a development of sequential analysis, taking account of longer sequences of events. The therapy session is segmented into units or stages that can be coded and these units are then related to outcomes. For example, Elliot et al. (2001) showed that the process by which therapist interpretation led to client insight was not just a simple sequence of one leading to the other, but rather a more prolonged and complex series of events. The interpretation was followed by the client thinking about the interpretation, coming to an initial insight, and then exploring the insight and elaborating on it.

Process research into career counselling

Unfortunately, this healthy attention to process variables in therapeutic counselling research has not been mirrored in studies evaluating career counselling. Most work appears to assume that career counselling is homogeneous in approach, yet we know that career counsellors differ in all kinds of ways, for example in their theoretical orientation, their attitude to offering occupational information, and the way they use assessment tools. However, there has recently been some recognition that career counsellors work in different ways, and this could affect outcomes. For example, in the US, Multon, Ellis-Kalton, Heppner and Gysbers (2003) assessed the extent to which the types of responses trainee career counsellors used were related to the development of a working alliance. They found that self disclosure by counsellors had a significantly negative relationship with the development of a working alliance. This was explained by the general lack of appropriateness of the self disclosures.

In another American example, Hanson, Claiborn and Kerr (1997) investigated the effects of two styles of test interpretation on clients' cognitive processing of the test results; evaluation of the career counselling session; and perceptions of their counsellor. The tests used were the Personality Research Form, a measure of personality, and the Vocational Preference Inventory, a measure of occupational interests. For one group of clients, test results were given in a way that allowed no discussion. For the other group, the results were given in an interactive way, involving the client in discussion throughout. Career counselling sessions in which interactive interpretations of test results were given were seen as having more impact and the counsellors were perceived to be more expert, trustworthy and attractive. There was no difference in the two groups in how they processed the test results.

Process evaluation work in the UK is very limited. One study, however, showed that helpful interventions, as perceived by counsellors and clients, were characterised by several features (Wilden & La Gro, 1998). These included: conveying that the client was understood; giving positive feedback about strengths; clear explanations about the conduct of the interview; systematic questioning; clarifying what the client meant; and insights leading to a re-interpretation or re-structuring of the situation.

Meta-analyses, or syntheses of research findings, are commonly carried out to review the evidence on the effectiveness of interventions. In a meta-analysis carried out by Brown et al. (2002), five critical ingredients of effective career interventions were identified:

- Workbooks that contain assignments and written exercises.
- Opportunities to gather and process information within a counselling session.
- Feedback of the results of assessment from a trained practitioner, with opportunities to integrate this into the self concept.
- Opportunities to interact with or observe appropriate models.
- Efforts to help the client build support networks.

Outcome Research

A key question in outcome research is: how much better off, in general, is a treated client than he or she would have been without treatment? The best way to assess this is to use an experimental design in which participants are randomly assigned to a treatment group and a non-treatment group. The treatment group receive the intervention, and the functioning of all participants is assessed either immediately afterwards or some time later.

Outcome research into therapeutic counselling

Smith and Glass (1977) conducted a meta-analysis of outcome studies of therapeutic counselling and psychotherapy. They reviewed 375 studies that compared a counselling or therapeutic treatment to a control group. The efficacy of treatment was assessed by calculating the *effect size* of the treatment (that is, the difference in the obtained sample means divided by the standard deviation of the control group). A positive effect size showed that the treatment was effective, and this was expressed in standard deviation units.

Because multiple outcome measures were used in some studies, the 375 studies produced 833 indices of effect size. The studies included over 25,000 control group and 25,000 treatment participants, and the mean effect size was 0.68. This means that the post-treatment outcome variable means of the treatment groups were overall superior to the post-treatment means of the control groups by 0.68 standard deviations. If one assumes that scores were normally distributed, this effect size of 0.68 can be interpreted as indicating that 75 per cent of those treated were better than the average of those not treated. They concluded that there was enough evidence to assert with some certainty that counselling and psychotherapy were helpful.

The work of Smith and Glass (1977) was an important contribution to knowledge in this area. Their findings have been criticised though, one criticism being that since many of the studies were flawed the estimate of the effect size was also flawed. However, Smith and Glass had taken some account of this, as they had examined various threats to the internal validities of the studies.

More recently, Wampold (2000) provided a comprehensive review of studies of what he calls the efficacy of counselling and psychotherapy. He posed the question: 'Are counselling and psychotherapy effective for all problems and disorders?' The answer is that for problems that are thought to be appropriate for treatment and which have been studied by researchers, counselling and psychotherapy are effective. Wampold's review showed that large effect sizes have been obtained across a range of problems, including depression, anxiety and marital problems.

It is important to note, however, that these are findings from clinical trials, which are artificial contexts. The results of clinical trials may not generalise to the settings in which counselling and psychotherapy are typically practised. The problem is, though, that random assignment to treatment and control groups is not normally possible in clinical settings. Wampold's (2000) work suggests that the evidence for effectiveness from practitioners' day-to-day work is somewhat weaker than the evidence from clinical trials.

Given that therapeutic counselling and psychotherapy appear to be effective, it is also necessary to identify, through process research, what components of treatment produce beneficial outcomes. Wampold (2000), along with others, suggests that the positive outcomes of the various treatments can be attributed to one of two sources: common factors or specific ingredients. The idea of common factors was discussed earlier, in Chapter 3, and it refers to a core set of non-specific elements of the counselling process that are beneficial to clients. The term 'specific ingredients' refers to those components of treatment that are considered unique to the treatment and essential (for example, in psychodynamic therapy, focusing on unconscious determinants of behaviour).

If all treatments produce the same sorts of outcome, then it is likely that common factors (for example, therapist warmth, opportunity for catharsis and the development of the working alliance) are likely to be the cause of the outcomes. (Although, it could, of course, be argued that it is the specific ingredients that produce change in the client, but all the ingredients are equally powerful.) On the other hand, if treatments using different approaches vary in their efficacy, this is likely to be due to the fact that the specific ingredients of some kinds of treatments are more potent than the specific ingredients of others. Overall, there is very little evidence that one approach to therapeutic counselling or psychotherapy is more effective than any other.

Outcome research into career counselling

We turn now to consider outcome research into the effectiveness of career counselling. Because many of the studies evaluating career counselling also assess the effectiveness of other types of career interventions (for example, career education), our discussion will also cover the evaluation of career interventions more broadly.

As a recent OECD report on guidance in the UK observed, much of the research that has been conducted evaluating the effectiveness of guidance has been 'one-off and fragmented, rather than strategic, and not disseminated widely or effectively' (OECD, 2003: 22). However, interest in the evidence underpinning practice has increased in recent years, for several reasons. First, there has been a concern from government departments about how far spending in this area can be justified. Secondly, there is more interest across public services generally in evidence-based practice. And thirdly there is a desire from researchers in the career counselling and guidance field for a more cohesive research community (Hawthorn, Killeen, Kidd & Watts, 2003).

Most studies evaluating career counselling have been conducted in the United States. As Killeen, Kidd, Watts and Hawthorn (2003) observed, the disparity in research output between the US and the UK is much larger than expected, given the relative size of the two countries. The reason for this is that institutions and agencies offering career support in the UK have not evolved in the same way or to the same degree as those in the US. While most evaluation in the US takes place as a branch of applied psychology, this is rare in the UK. Another problem with UK evaluation research identified by Killeen et al. (2003) is that too few of those who commission and carry out evaluations are aware of the accumulated body of knowledge and there is a high turnover of the people who commission and conduct evaluation research. The research therefore lacks a 'collective memory'. Also, findings from studies are often incapable of generalisation to other contexts.

In contrast to researchers in therapeutic counselling, those evaluating career counselling have put considerable effort into establishing what the appropriate outcomes of career counselling might, or should, be. One reason for this is that most career guidance and counselling services in the UK are funded by the state, and so they are under pressure to produce benefits to both government and individuals. This increases the range of potential outcomes of career counselling, and also highlights issues to do with the relative importance of different outcomes. Individual clients, for example, may value help with long-term career planning, while the government policy imperative may be to reduce unemployment. In contrast, a greater proportion of therapeutic counselling services are independent, and there is therefore less pressure to demonstrate benefits beyond client improvement. Another reason for debates about relevant outcomes is that different career counselling approaches have different purposes, as we have seen earlier.

Potential outcomes of career counselling

Career counselling potentially leads to a range of outcomes (Killeen, 1996). These can be grouped into the following categories:

- Immediate outcomes, for example, the learning outcomes of self and opportunity awareness, and changes in attitudes and motivation in relation to work.
- Intermediate outcomes, for example, better job search skills, and a wider exploration of opportunities.
- Ultimate outcomes at the individual level, for example, suitable career choices, and enhanced take up of learning and work opportunities.
- Ultimate outcomes at the system level, for example, increased labour productivity.

Immediate and intermediate outcomes

Learning outcomes have been defined by Kidd and Killeen (1992: 221) as 'the skills, knowledge and attitudes which facilitate rational occupational and educational decision making and the effective implementation of occupational and educational decisions.'

One frequently used classification of learning outcomes in the UK is Law and Watts' (1977) four-fold scheme, often referred to as the DOTS framework. This sets out the four aims of career guidance (and therefore the kinds of outcome that should be evaluated) as follows:

- Decision learning – the awareness and skills required to make informed reasoned decisions.
- Opportunity awareness – understanding the structure of the working world and the opportunities within it.
- Transition learning – the awareness and skills needed to implement decisions and to cope with their consequences.
- Self-awareness – understanding individual strengths, interests and needs.

The evidence for immediate and intermediate outcomes
Learning outcomes and other types of immediate and intermediate outcomes have come to be used as a result of the shift towards a more developmental orientation to career guidance and counselling, in contrast to simple person–environment fit approaches. As Kidd and Killeen (1992) have pointed out, it is somewhat easier to assess these outcomes than career states. For example, post-intervention measurements can be made soon after the intervention, and there is a realistic prospect of showing significant effects in small samples.

Literally hundreds of studies evaluating the effectiveness of career interventions on these kinds of outcomes have been carried out over the last few decades, most of them in the United States and most using an experimental design. A recent meta-analysis of career interventions is that of Whiston, Sexton and Lasoff (1998), and it will be instructive to examine the findings of this work in some detail.

Whiston et al. (1998) were interested in finding out which kinds of career interventions are effective for which clients under what circumstances. They examined the findings of 46 studies, all of which involved a comparison between a career-intervention treatment group and a control group. Each study involved an average of 99 participants, and the effect size was calculated for each.

The average effect size over all the studies, adjusted for small sample bias, was 0.30. This was interpreted as moderate to small. Overall, the career interventions were most effective for young people in their early teens (effect size = 0.79). Interestingly, the most effective interventions were those carried out by trainee career counsellors (effect size = 0.51). Whiston et al. (1998) suggest that one reason for trainee career counsellors being more effective is because they are more closely supervised than those with more experience. Also, they receive more specific instructions concerning career counselling techniques.

The studies in this meta-analysis covered a range of different types of career interventions. These included: individual career counselling; group career counselling; group test interpretation; workshops; career education in the classroom; computer interventions; and counsellor-free interventions. Individual career counselling produced the largest effect size (0.75), and it was also found to produce the most gain per hour of session. Moreover, the effects of individual career counselling occurred quite quickly: the mean number of hours to achieve this large effect was 2.5. It should be noted though that only three studies of individual career counselling were included in the meta-analysis. The most efficient treatment (judged by the ratio of effectiveness to number of clients) was computer-delivered career interventions.

Almost all the studies assessed learning outcomes, rather than more ultimate career outcomes. The most common outcome categories were: career information seeking; certainty-decidedness; traditionality of choice (one of the few career outcomes); career skills; and career maturity. The most effective interventions were those intended to improve career skills, such as interviewing and CV writing skills (effect size = 0.81). Career maturity had the next largest effect size (0.53).

Whiston, Brecheisen and Stephens' (2003) later meta-analysis confirmed that counsellor-free career interventions were less effective than interventions that involved a counsellor. Furthermore, computer interventions were more effective when the computer activities were supplemented by counselling.

One potential problem with meta-analyses like these that only gather together the findings of published research, is that they may draw on a biased group of studies. Researchers are more likely to submit papers for publication, and more likely to have papers accepted for publication, if they describe positive results. This has been called the 'file-drawer problem': a reference to the potential existence of papers describing non-significant results that have never reached the journals, and instead lie unread in someone's filing cabinet.

In an attempt to counter this criticism, Whiston et al. (1998) calculated that over 14,000 studies with null findings would need to be hidden away in some metaphoric filing cabinet for their findings to be reduced to negligible effect sizes. They therefore concluded that the effect size for career interventions is resistant to the file-drawer problem.

Less evidence is available from the UK, but a range of studies is suggestive of the benefits of career support in these terms (see, for example, Killeen & White, 2000 and Tyers & Sinclair, 2005). The latter study compared outcomes experienced by a sample of over 2,000 individuals who received advice and guidance with the outcomes experienced by roughly the same number receiving information only. The advice and guidance group were significantly more likely to have started looking for a job, to find planning their future steps easier and to feel more confident and informed about their next move. They also were more likely to find learning about new things enjoyable and say that information about courses was easy to find.

Ultimate outcomes at the individual
and system level
These categories of outcomes refer to longer-term effects on individuals and on society as a whole. At the individual level examples refer to educational and career benefits for individuals, such as take-up of education and training, job satisfaction and less time spent unemployed. At the system level, there are potential effects on the economy, for example, reduction in skills shortages, and reduced recruitment and labour costs for employers.

Evaluation studies assessing ultimate outcomes, at least at the individual level, have a long history. As we saw in Chapter 2, during the early part of the twentieth century, the theoretical base for career support was person–environment fit theory. Practitioners' main task was to describe and assess individual differences and the characteristics of occupations in order to make recommendations about appropriate jobs.

The evidence for ultimate outcomes

The earliest studies evaluating career interventions were concerned primarily to establish how far individuals who entered jobs that were in accord with the recommendations were satisfied and successful in their work. However, these studies did not directly evaluate the effects of the help received: they were instead examining the predictive validity of the careers adviser's diagnostic judgement. Although there was ample evidence for effectiveness in these terms, it was impossible to judge whether clients would have been any less likely to enter appropriate occupations had they not received career guidance (Watts & Kidd, 1978).

Some of the first studies of the effectiveness of career interventions to use experimental designs were specifically concerned with assessing the effects of adding psychometric tests to the other techniques used. For example, Hunt and Smith (1944), showed that school-leavers whose advice was based on the results of tests were more likely to enter jobs in accordance with the advice received, and were more likely to be rated as suited to their jobs by their employers, and to rate themselves as suited to them.

It is important to note that these early studies were not concerned with *how* career decisions were made (for example, whether they were informed by knowledge of self and occupations); indeed clients' career decisions were essentially made for them by careers advisers. The outcome criteria used were subsequent career states.

Other 'ultimate' outcomes at the individual level include participation in education and training, educational attainment, performance at work and career progression. Some work suggests that career support leads to increased participation in learning. For example, the work by Tyers and Sinclair (2005), mentioned above, showed that the group of individuals receiving advice and guidance were more likely to have enrolled on a course and to be working towards a qualification than those receiving information only.

With regard to reduction in time spent unemployed, evidence from the US suggests that job clubs reduce unemployment (Azrin, Flores & Kaplan, 1975), but this intervention is much broader than career counselling, involving a range of activities aimed to encourage job search.

So far in this chapter we have discussed the outcomes of career counselling in terms of changes observed in individual clients. However, as indicated earlier, career support is generally regarded as a public as well as a private good. Watts and Sultana (2004) suggest that policy makers expect services providing career support to address three main categories of public policy goal. The first of these is *learning* goals, and this includes increasing the efficiency of the education and training system and its relationship to the labour market. The second is *labour market* goals, for example improving the match between supply and demand. Thirdly is the category of *social equity* goals, for example promoting equal opportunities and social inclusion. Also, from the point of view of employing organisations, goals might include increased organisational productivity, and fewer skill shortages.

The evidence for these kinds of ultimate goals and outcomes relies mainly on demonstrations that effects on individuals eventually impact on labour market processes. As Killeen (1996) has argued, the future of career guidance provision, particularly publicly funded services, will depend to a large degree on the advantages it offers to institutions and organisations and its 'public' or 'social' returns. For example, even a marginal impact on GDP would be enough to justify the modest level of public investment in career guidance and counselling.

Evidence for these ultimate economic benefits is lacking. However, Killeen's (1996) analysis suggests that if it can be shown that immediate effects of guidance are predictive of these kinds of ultimate economic benefits, we would have a strong case for greater public investment in career guidance and counselling services. What are needed, therefore, are longitudinal studies that measure each type of effect and which therefore allow conclusions to be drawn about the progressive impact of the interventions.

Epistemological and Methodological Issues

Most of the research discussed so far in this chapter adheres to a positivist paradigm, in that it assumes that there is one reality above and beyond our experience of it, and that this reality can be captured through direct objective observation. It also assumes that the aim of research is to understand the world through scientific laws. Variables are therefore quantified and carefully measured, with the researcher taking a detached, objective role.

Other studies, however, have been carried out within interpretive or constructivist paradigms, which assume that there are as many realities as there are people. In these studies, qualitative methods are used (for example, interviews) and the research process aims to gain an in-depth understanding of individuals' experiences. For example, Knox, Hess, Petersen and Hill (2001) asked clients about their experiences of helpful therapist self-disclosures, for example what therapists told them about their own personal experiences. They found that these disclosures often led to new insights and resulted in clients feeling more reassured.

The split between these approaches to research in counselling and psychotherapy has been a considerable source of conflict. It would seem that the disciplines that have had most influence on counselling have been psychology and psychiatry, and these disciplines have traditionally been associated with quantitative research. However, qualitative researchers hold values which are rather closer to those of most counselling practitioners, and this has led to a call for more qualitative research into both therapeutic counselling and career counselling (Collin, 1996; McLeod, 2001).

So why not combine quantitative and qualitative approaches? This may not be as straightforward as it seems. Some writers argue that because the premises of positivist and constructivist paradigms are mutually exclusive and philosophically contradictory, it may not be possible to simply pick and choose methods to use from each paradigm simultaneously (see, for example, Lincoln & Guba, 2000). They take the view that choice of research paradigm is more a matter of ontology and epistemology (how we view reality and knowledge) than of methodology. Others, however, assert that different research methods can bring different perspectives, and therefore enhance our understanding. Ponterotto and Grieger (1999), for example, argue that using a range of methods in social research is similar to becoming bi-cultural, since the different 'worldviews' within each approach bring complementary perspectives to the research. It might also be argued that for most researchers, choice of method is more a matter of the training they have experienced rather than a view of the nature of reality. With our current state of knowledge in the field of counselling, therefore, both approaches have much to offer, and in embracing new methodologies we must take care not to lose sight of the traditional positivist approaches which have informed this field since its beginning (Kidd, 2004).

Summary

In this chapter we have discussed research into the effectiveness of both therapeutic and career counselling. There is an important distinction to be made between process research and outcome research. The former focuses on the factors that lead to benefits for the client, and the latter on whether and how far interventions help clients. Process research, although limited, has suggested some key features of effective career interventions: written exercises; opportunities to gather and process information; feedback from assessment; contact with models; and help in building networks. Outcome research has demonstrated the effectiveness of career counselling, at least when assessed in terms of immediate and intermediate outcomes, such as career maturity and career information-seeking. However, evidence for longer term effects is lacking at present. There have been calls for more qualitative research, but both quantitative and qualitative methods have value in research into the benefits of career counselling.

Discuss and Debate

1   Drawing on the material in earlier chapters, what do you consider to be the most important outcome criteria to use in evaluating career counselling?

2   What kind of research study would add most to our understanding of what career counsellors need to do to maximise their effectiveness?

3   Design a study to establish how far the clients of a career counselling service benefit from career counselling. Defend your use of the research methods you suggest.

PART TWO   PRACTICE

FIVE   The Career Counselling Process and the Skills Involved

The focus in this chapter is on the process of career counselling, as it is manifest in the flow of career counselling sessions with the client. A four stage model of career counselling is introduced, with associated tasks. We also consider how the various theoretical orientations to career counselling discussed earlier fit with the process model outlined in this chapter. A range of basic career counselling skills is then outlined.

The Stages and Tasks of Career Counselling

Our approach here draws on Egan's (2002) three-stage model of helping (described in Chapter 3): identifying and clarifying problem situations and unused opportunities; developing a preferred scenario; and formulating strategies and plans. The model we will use, however, extends into four stages, and places rather more emphasis on the early tasks of clarifying clients' needs and identifying best how to proceed. The model is described in Table 5.1.

The career counselling process is seen as comprising four stages: building the relationship; enabling clients' self-understanding; exploring new perspectives; and forming strategies and plans. This is an over-simple model of what actually happens in career counselling – usually sessions will move back and forth between these stages – but it serves to illustrate some of the key activities. It should be borne in mind, though, that not everyone who seeks help with career issues will want to or need to go through the whole process of career counselling. Some people will only need limited help: for example, with obtaining some specific career information and relating it to their career plans. Other clients, although they would benefit from participating in the full process over a period

Table 5.1 The stages and associated tasks of career counselling

Stages	Tasks
1 Building the relationship	Establishing the working alliance
2 Enabling clients' self-understanding	Assessment
3 Exploring new perspectives	Challenging and information giving
4 Forming strategies and plans	Reviewing progress and goal setting

Source: Kidd (2003: 471)

of time, may be resistant to doing this. Dealing with this resistance is likely to be a priority in the early stages of career counselling, when the working alliance is being developed.

Two of the tasks – assessment and information giving – are particularly important in career counselling and they merit a more extended discussion. Accordingly, these topics will be explored in more depth in Chapters 6 and 7.

Stage 1: Building the relationship

As we saw earlier, in the discussion of person–environment fit approaches to career counselling, the image of the career counsellor as an 'expert', offering advice and recommendations on suitable jobs, is an enduring one. Moreover, many clients expect career counselling to consist mainly of information about occupations, careers and educational courses, and are disappointed when they do not receive this. At the outset, therefore, it is important to help clients understand that career counselling is a collaborative venture, and that they need to be an active participant at every stage.

As Nathan and Hill (2006) suggest, clients can be helped to have realistic expectations of career counselling even before the two parties meet. A telephone conversation, for example, can help to identify and minimise misunderstandings, or written information can be sent to the client. Also, agreeing a client–counsellor 'contract' is crucial in the first session. Issues of confidentiality, and the number, length and frequency of meetings will need to be discussed, but more generally the nature of the counselling process itself will need covering, as will the techniques that might be used, and the limits of the relationship. These can be summarised within each stage as:

- Goals – what is the aim of the relationship, the aim of this particular phase or session, or the aim of working on this particular issue?
- Roles – who is doing what and who is responsible for what?
- Tasks – what are the tasks of this particular stage?

'Contracting' can be seen as a process that runs throughout the career counselling relationship, designed to minimise discrepancies between the views of the two parties. Above all, it is a joint process where both parties express their views and make requests and suggestions.

The importance of agreeing a contract to the success of helping relationships is asserted in a considerable body of literature. Bordin (1979) was among the first to use the term 'working alliance' to describe the quality of the early relationship between the counsellor and the client. From a psychoanalytic perspective, Bordin saw the working alliance as arising out of the transference relationship that the client develops with the counsellor. However, he also emphasised its importance in other helping settings, including teaching and group work.

The contract may need to be renegotiated several times during the course of career counselling. Agreeing a contract and renegotiating it may seem fairly straightforward, but research with careers advisers suggests that many are unclear and confused about what the contract should consist of. They are also concerned that the contract could come to dominate the career counselling session, particularly where it was relatively short (Kidd, Killeen, Jarvis & Offer, 1997).

Considering the client's cultural origin may be particularly important in agreeing a contract. Clients from cultures that place importance on respect for authority may find it difficult to accept that they should take responsibility for their decision making. Moreover, clients from cultures where family and group responsibilities take precedence over individual needs may not find it easy to engage in self-reflection.

Apart from explicitly agreeing a contract, there are practical strategies that the practitioner can use to establish and maintain a strong working alliance with the client. McLeod's (2003) suggestions include adopting a collaborative style by using 'metacommunication'. This involves standing back from the communication process in order to assess it and reviewing the relationship when counselling becomes 'stuck', perhaps by drawing attention to what is happening in the here-and-now relationship, for example by asking 'I have a sense that you are withdrawing from me. Am I right?'

Stage 2: Enabling clients' self-understanding

In the second stage of the helping process the main task is to help clients deepen their understanding and insight into their situation and the issues that are concerning them. Many clients will gain important insights through the counselling process itself, and this will often be sufficient for progress to be made. However, it is often useful to make use of more structured assessment techniques and tools. Clearly, each client will have unique needs. Some types of techniques will work well with some clients and yet be unhelpful to others, and certain attributes will need particular attention in one situation and different attributes in another.

Much of the value of assessment techniques at this stage is that they help clients become familiar with conceptual frameworks to organise their knowledge of themselves and their situation. Simple self-assessment tools, as well as knowledge gained through the interview itself, often produce insights which are just as illuminating as those gained from administering psychometric tests and inventories.

A model set out by Law and Ward (1981), derived from person–environment fit theories, is helpful in identifying some of the types of attributes that clients may be helped to assess. Law and Ward's basic point is that two main criteria inform the process of choice: performance criteria and motivational criteria. Performance criteria are used in attempting to match the talents of the individual to the demands of opportunities, and motivational criteria are used in matching the needs, values and interests of the individual to the incentives and rewards of particular job opportunities. Law and Ward also distinguish between the different locations upon which attention is focused: self and situation. Their model is set out in Table 5.2.

Table 5.2   Processes of career development

Criteria controlling the processes	Location of material informing the processes	
	In the person	*In the situation*
Performance	Process 1: 'What have I (has he or she) to offer?'	Process 2: 'What tasks are there for me (him or her) to perform?'
Motivation	Process 3: 'What satisfactions do I (does he or she) seek?'	Process 4: 'What incentives and rewards are there for me (him or her) in the work?'

Note: The numbering of processes is for convenience of reference and is not meant to imply sequence.

Source: Law and Ward (1981: 104)

This analysis helps in distinguishing two important categories of attributes: strengths and weaknesses; and interests and values. The term 'strengths and weaknesses' is used very broadly here, to refer to what the individual has to offer. This category includes aptitudes, attainments, personality characteristics and physical attributes. As we saw in Chapter 1, the term interests refers to people's preferences for particular work activities. Values refer to basic beliefs about what is important to the individual.

In Chapter 6 we will describe some techniques that can be used to help clients assess their attributes.

Stage 3: Exploring new perspectives

Challenging

It will often be important to help clients develop and explore new perspectives on their problems, by sensitively helping them confront self-defeating behaviours or ways in which they may be preventing themselves from moving on. As Nathan and Hill (2006) argue, sound counselling skills are essential throughout this process, especially the skills of identifying life themes and patterns. Counsellor interventions which challenge or confront clients' beliefs are usually only appropriate some way into the counselling process and should only be attempted once a trusting relationship has been established. Dryden (1979) and Mitchell and Krumboltz (1996) see challenging clients' irrational thinking and inaccurate beliefs as key tasks in career counselling. Dryden argues that the literature on rational-emotive therapy suggests useful techniques for challenging, while Mitchell and Krumboltz argue the case for challenging from the perspective of social learning theory. In the latter part of their chapter, they suggest several guidelines for identifying 'problematic' beliefs:

- Examine the assumptions and presuppositions of the expressed belief.
- Look for inconsistencies between words and actions.
- Test simplistic answers for inadequacies.
- Confront attempts to build an illogical consistency.
- Identify barriers to the goal.
- Challenge the validity of key beliefs.

Information-giving

The vast range of information about the world of work, much of which is constantly being updated, means that it is virtually impossible for career counsellors to keep up to date with information about opportunities, even in one specific area. Accordingly, and as Nathan and Hill (2006) suggest, it is more appropriate for career counsellors to view themselves as 'general practitioners' with respect to knowledge of occupational and educational opportunities. Clearly, this is more in line with the career counsellor's facilitative role, too.

Nevertheless, it will be important for career counsellors to possess some knowledge of how to access career information, labour market information (including trends in the demand for labour), the frameworks used to describe work and occupations and information about specific opportunities. We will discuss the use of information in career counselling in Chapter 7, focusing particularly on the constructs and frameworks used to describe work. Labour market information is readily available from government sources (for example, the publication Labour Market Trends), and information about specific opportunities will be specific to career counsellors' working environments, and it is therefore difficult to discuss in general terms.

Stage 4: Forming strategies and plans

Reviewing progress

Reviewing progress is likely to be an integral part of the career counselling process at various stages, but particularly near the end. It may also be necessary to revisit and review the counselling 'contract' at certain points. Setting time aside for a review may be particularly useful in highlighting areas where progress has been made.

Goal setting

A key activity in preparing for the end of the career counselling relationship is helping clients set goals and decide on the steps they need to take to achieve those goals. The production of 'action plans' has been seen as one of the main tangible outcomes of career guidance provided to school leavers in the UK.

Goal-setting theory has been applied to the action-planning stage of career counselling, and Miller, Crute and Hargie (1992) have set out what this theory suggests as the main features of an effective goal:

- Clear and behaviourally specific
- Measurable
- Achievable
- Owned by the goal setter
- Congruent with his or her values
- Appropriately time scaled

Some approaches to career counselling, however, see the *whole* intervention largely in terms of goal setting. Mitchell and Krumboltz's (1996) social learning approach, Egan's (2002) model of helping, and Miller et al.'s (1992) model of the interview as an interpersonal interaction are examples.

Once a goal has been agreed, clients can be encouraged to develop an action plan. Nathan and Hill (2006) argue that an action plan is more likely to be successful if the following criteria are met:

- Goals are well-thought through
- The action plan is owned by the client
- The client understands that the plan is not rigid
- The client is prepared to review the plan regularly
- Enough time is given to address the fear of change
- Ways of coping with disappointment are identified

It is often helpful to arrange a review meeting some time after the last career counselling session to discuss progress.

One technique that may be useful in action planning is force-field analysis. This involves the following steps:

1 Clients are asked to list all the restraining forces or constraints that they might experience during the implementation of their action plans (for example, their lack of skills, other people's reactions).
2 They then list all the facilitating forces or resources that could contribute to the development of the action plan.

3   The most significant forces in each list are then identified.
4   Clients then identify ways of lessening the impact of the restraining
    forces and maximising the effects of the facilitating forces.

Prompts that the career counsellors might use to facilitate this
process include: Who might help? What have others done in similar situations? Where might help be available? And what things might help
(for example, training, books, equipment)?

Career Counselling Skills

As we saw earlier, the main aim of this text is to introduce you to the
theoretical background to career counselling, and the nature of the
career counselling process. The text cannot in itself provide training in
the skills of career counselling: for this students need to participate in
a face-to-face course. This is because these skills cannot be learned simply
by reading about them; students need to practise them with clients and
receive feedback from tutors.

Nevertheless, in order to fully appreciate the nature of the career
counselling process it is necessary to understand some core counselling
and helping skills and how they can be used in career counselling. Most
recent writers in the field take the view that a range of basic helping skills
is common to all approaches to career counselling. However, the mix
of skills used depend on theoretical orientation: cognitive-behavioural
approaches emphasise challenging skills more than other approaches,
for example. We have covered the main skills that are unique to particular approaches earlier. In this section, therefore, we will describe
the main generic helping skills.

One of the approaches to counselling that pays particular attention
to the quality of the counselling relationship and the skills that communicate
that relationship is the person-centred approach. In Chapter 3 we discussed
the three 'necessary and sufficient conditions' outlined by Rogers (1957):
congruence; unconditional positive regard; and empathic understanding.
A useful model of these skills has been developed by Ali and Graham (1996)
(see Figure 5.1). This shows that some skills are more fundamental than
others, although all are essential within a helping relationship.

At the base of the pyramid are the fundamental skills of *active listening*. Active listening means listening to the content of what is being
said, how it is said, possible meanings behind the words, and the feelings expressed.

At the next level are *understanding* skills, including the skills of restat-
ing, summarising, paraphrasing and using open questions. These skills
are sometimes referred to as reflective skills. One important objective
here is to develop empathy with the client as he or she is encouraged to
review, examine and understand what they are saying and how they feel.
As Ali and Graham (1996) observe, it is important not to underestimate

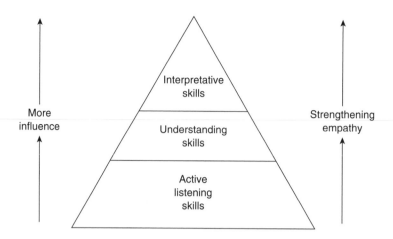

Figure 5.1 The skills pyramid

Source: Ali and Graham (1996)

the power of feeling understood by another person. When using these understanding skills it is essential that the fundamental listening skills are in place, since understanding cannot happen without listening.

At the highest level of the pyramid are *interpretative* skills. These include challenging, immediacy (drawing attention to what is happening here and now in the interview) and self-disclosure. These are called interpretative skills because in using them, the career counsellor is conveying his or her interpretation of the issues that are concerning the client. A strong level of empathy needs to have been developed before these skills can be used, and the career counsellor should maintain and develop that empathy by continuing to use listening and understanding skills. So the career counsellor uses fundamental listening skills throughout the whole process; introduces understanding skills to help clarify issues; and only starts to use interpretative skills much later, and perhaps not until several career counselling sessions have taken place.

As the career counselling relationship develops and the skills at higher levels in the pyramid come into play, the career counsellor is seen to have a greater influence on the direction of the process.

The skills pyramid in action

We can get a better feel for what is involved in some of these skills by looking at two of the examples set out by Ali and Graham (1996). The following exchange shows how paraphrasing is used to convey the gist of what the client has said:

> This client is describing her perceptions of teaching as a career after work-shadowing in her own old secondary school. She is now unsure if teaching is for her.

Mary: It was a bit strange – I got on really well with the kids; they were very chatty. The teacher (he had taught me) was very encouraging, I suppose. He even let me teach a lesson, but I was very uncomfortable about it.

Adviser: It sounds as if you were uncomfortable about teaching in front of your ex-teacher.

Mary: Yes. And I was always a bit in awe of that teacher. He kept impressing on me how hard he has to work. Then he started to push me to work with the sixth-year class every week. I wanted to help, but this is my final year and I have my dissertation to complete.

Adviser: So you feel pressurised by this teacher to take on some work you do not really have time for?

Mary: That's right. Then he began to imply that I would never get on a teacher training course if I did not help out. I did not plan to get so involved at this point, you know. I have other ideas I want to check out. I just wanted to get a flavour of what the job is all about.

*Adviser
[reflecting
feeling]:*   You sound angry when you say that.

Mary: Yes. Angry and used. Perhaps it was a mistake to go back to my old school. I might get a clearer picture if I try a different school.

Through paraphrasing and reflecting feeling, the counsellor enables the client to clarify what it is about the experience that has coloured her view of teaching. The client feels understood; she is enabled to express her feelings, and to begin to recognise her more 'adult' role as teacher and the difficulty of trying out that role in a place where she still felt like a pupil. (Ali & Graham, 1996: 71–2)

In the next excerpt from a career counselling interview, Ali and Graham (1996) show how an open question can be asked in a tentative manner:

Lydia: I just don't know what to do. If I take a job abroad, I would leave my mother on her own. She has been widowed just a few months. I'm not sure any job is worth it. I haven't even had the courage to tell her about it yet. On the other hand, I'd be denying myself a tremendous opportunity – I expect she wouldn't want me to lose that.

Adviser: You sound apprehensive about how your mother will react when you tell her. How do you imagine she will be?

With this question, the adviser moves the client along in the process by encouraging her to imagine herself in the difficult situation. It may allow her to explore more fully what is holding her back from making a decision (e.g. fear of her mother dying too, of her own personal fear about tackling a new culture on her own). (Ali & Graham, 1996: 75)

Although identifying specific skills is helpful in conceptualising client–counsellor interactions, particularly for the purposes of initial training, it has been suggested that looking at counsellor behaviour in this way is inappropriate. McLeod (2003) argues that many of the key abilities of the counsellor involve internal, unobservable processes. For example, an effective counsellor is likely to be aware of how he or she feels in the presence of the client, and this is not easily understood by observing the skills used. Furthermore, effective counsellors are able to view their own actions, and those of the client, in the total context of the counselling relationship. It is argued therefore that it is inappropriate to assess the 'skilfulness' of the intervention by dividing it into micro-elements. McLeod also argues that personal qualities, for example genuineness, are just as important as skills.

In addition to the helping skills described above, it is suggested that effective career counsellors are likely to display the following qualities:

- Openness, to other people, and to knowledge.
- Emotional stability and self awareness.
- Conceptual ability, in the sense of understanding issues in terms of abstract concepts and conceptual frameworks.
- Capacity for critical thinking and to challenge accepted knowledge and beliefs.

Research is needed to assess the importance of these qualities and to identify others that impact on the effectiveness of career counselling.

Summary

We have seen in this chapter that the career counselling process can be considered as a series of stages and associated tasks. The first is building the relationship and the main task in this stage involves establishing a working alliance with the client. The second stage is enabling clients' self-understanding; assessment tools and techniques are frequently used in this stage. At the third stage, exploring new perspectives, one important task is likely to involve challenging the client, by helping them deal with behaviours that may be preventing them dealing with career issues. Another is information giving. The fourth stage, forming strategies and plans, involves reviewing progress and goal setting.

Career counselling involves many of the same skills as those used in therapeutic counselling. Basic career counselling skills include active listening, understanding and interpretative skills, but it is argued that other qualities are important too, particularly openness, emotional stability and awareness, conceptual ability and the capacity for critical thinking.

Discuss and Debate

1 To what extent are the techniques used in rational-emotive therapy for challenging irrational thinking in conflict with the person-centred approach?
2 What would a good action plan look like? How useful are action plans in career counselling?
3 Reflect on your experiences of getting support from a sympathetic person. What skills did that person display? Do they differ from those discussed in this chapter?

SIX   Assessment Tools and Techniques

In this chapter we discuss some of the main tools and techniques used in assessment and ways to use them in career counselling. Assessment involves the gathering of evidence about individuals in order to help them manage their careers. As we saw in Chapter 1, the person–environment fit approach dominated career assessment during the last century. Changes in the context in which careers are experienced, particularly the increased diversity of career patterns, have meant assessment is now used less for suggesting and predicting suitable occupations, and more for broader explorations about values, needs and areas for self-development. Arguably, it is in this area of career counselling practice that the greatest divide exists between researchers and practitioners. Practitioners' awareness of the instruments available is often limited because they may be unable to access key journals and many lack the training to make an informed assessment of a particular instrument. This review of tools and techniques will hopefully help to increase career counsellors' knowledge of the area and encourage them to seek further training.

The review is organised in terms of the degree of formality and standardisation of the tools described. We begin with relatively informal procedures, continue with a description of standardised inventories and tests, and conclude with a discussion of how to use assessment in career counselling.

Career counsellors often use these tools and techniques as home assignments between counselling sessions. Nathan and Hill (2006) see home assignments as having several general purposes.

- Maintaining continuity and interest, forming a bridge between sessions.
- Giving clients opportunities to explore an issue in more depth.
- Reinforcing the idea that career counselling is a process, rather than an event.
- Encouraging the client to be an active, responsible participant in counselling.
- Providing information about the client from the way a task is approached.

In relation to the last purpose, Nathan and Hill describe how the manner in which clients present their work is sometimes as revealing as its content, and this can suggest important counselling issues. For example:

> Stella came in for her session rather breathless and dishevelled, saying 'I didn't have much time to get those exercises done!' She scrabbled about in the bottom of an untidy briefcase to retrieve several dog-eared sheets covered in scrawled notes. Her chaotic approach to the exercise reflected the chaos of her life, both in and out of work. (Nathan and Hill, 2006: 52)

Systematic Reflection on Experience

In essence, this technique involves encouraging clients to analyse their past experiences to discover what can be learned from them. It draws on Kolb's (1976) model of experiential learning, which he describes as a process comprising four stages:

1 Concrete experience.
2 Reflective observation.
3 Abstract conceptualisation.
4 Active experimentation.

At each stage, different demands are placed on individuals. At the first stage, 'concrete experience', it is argued that learners should involve themselves fully and openly in new experiences. During the second stage, 'reflective observation', they should step back and reflect on the experience. At the 'abstract conceptualisation' stage they should attempt to understand and theoretically integrate these observations. Lastly, during 'active experimentation', they should plan the next steps by testing out what they have learned and using it as a basis for planning what to do next.

This model is used in the technique of systematic reflection on experience in the following way. First, clients are asked to reflect on an experience, for example, a job they have had in the past or a leisure interest. They are then asked to:

- Review the experience, by describing how they performed the activity, and the satisfactions they sought and achieved.
- Conclude from the experience, by describing what they feel they learned about their abilities, values, personality etc. from the activity.
- Plan the next steps, by identifying other situations to which that learning may be appropriate and describing how they might generalise the learning to these situations.

The following example (Kidd, 1988) may help to illustrate the process:

> Jean is a thirty-five year-old woman who has spent the last fifteen years looking after her family and home. She very much wants to return to paid employment, but says she has no particular skills or qualifications, having done only unskilled factory work before having her children. When asked about her work experience, she says 'None – I have only been a housewife'. It has never occurred to Jean that the tasks of running a home and caring for children involve a considerable number of skills which may be transferable to paid employment and to other life roles.
>
> The guidance worker attempts to help Jean reflect on the tasks she has been carrying out over the last fifteen years.

Guidance	
Worker (G.W.):	Shall we have a look at the things that are involved in looking after a home and family? Perhaps we could make a list.
Jean:	Well there is shopping, cooking, housework, trying to get by with my weekly housekeeping money, getting the children to do their homework, looking after the children when they are ill ... (Jean lists 15 tasks).
G.W.:	Good. Now let's try to pick out some of the things from the list that you feel you do well, the things you feel satisfied with and proud of.
Jean:	I suppose I do pride myself on getting through the week and having a bit of money over. I quite like shopping around for bargains, I pay all the bills, too, in our house, you know, the electricity bill, the gas bill, and I see to the income tax forms – my husband says I am good with figures so he leaves it all to me.
G.W.:	There seem to be quite a few things there that you seem to be good at. You're good at managing money, good at working with figures. Do you think that's true of you generally?
Jean:	I don't know, I was never much good at maths at school, but thinking about it I suppose it is – I do quite enjoy numbers – I used to help the children with their maths when they were younger.
G.W.:	Do you think, then, that perhaps you would enjoy a job that involved working with figures ...? (Kidd, 1988: 28)

Although it gives a very simplified view of the process, this example shows how it is possible to help people identify transferable skills (generic skills which can be used in a range of settings, for example, problem solving, numeracy and team work) through reflecting on various activities and experiences. One advantage of this approach is that it helps focus on strengths rather than weaknesses. As we saw in Chapter 1, proponents of social cognitive career theory argue that helping clients increase their perceptions of self-efficacy can be particularly beneficial. However, the technique is not only applicable in identifying skills; it is equally useful in helping clients think about other attributes, such as personality and interests and, more broadly, what practitioners taking a narrative perspective call career or life-career themes.

Assessing career themes

As shown in Chapter 3, practitioners using narrative approaches often focus on identifying career or life-career themes in career counselling. Life-career themes have been described as 'the ways people express ideas, beliefs, attitudes, and values about themselves, others, and the world – in general, their world views' (Gysbers, Heppner & Johnson, 2003).

Gysbers et al. (2003) suggest that clients' approaches towards work and social relationships can be analysed in this way, and they provide a useful guide to an interview structure based on this approach. This is a task shared between client and counsellor that helps clients understand their 'unique sense of the meaning of life' (Gysbers et al., 2003: 182). This sounds like rather an ambitious goal, but more prosaically it is a technique that can often lead to useful in-depth discussion of perceived strengths and weaknesses, values and interests. Their suggested 'Life Career Assessment' interview structure involves discussing:

- Work experience and education and training, including what was most and least liked.
- Leisure activities.
- A typical day, including how far the individual relies on others or is more independent, and how far they like routine or spontaneity.
- Strengths and obstacles.

Recurring themes from the dialogue are identified and shared with the client. The following excerpt from a 'Life Career Assessment' interview is from Gysbers et al. (2003):

Counselor: When you think back to elementary school, you said you liked it pretty well. What were some things you remember liking, what was good?

Client: Um, I can remember third and fourth grade … spelling and capitalisation and stuff like that. We always had special games to make it a lot more fun, you know. The spelling bee. If you completed so many words right we got a star on the board. Things like that. I remember how the teacher always pointed me out as being the one person who always got the stars. I guess the things I got rewards for made it more interesting.

(Possible themes: seeks rewards and recognition. Approval from adults is important.)

Counselor: You felt like you could see that you had done something good …
Client: She would have me help other people.

(Possible theme: seeks acceptance.) (Gysbers et al., 2003: 186)

These potential themes would need to be discussed and checked with the client later in the interview.

Graphic and Written Portrayals

Here, clients are asked to portray themselves graphically or in writing. Some clients find it easier to express themselves using diagrams rather than words, particularly when they wish to explore ideas and feelings which may be hard to verbalise. These approaches may be good starting points for reflecting on past experience, setting future goals and analysing strengths and weaknesses. For example:

- 'Road maps' and 'life-lines' can be used to help clients review their life up to the present or into the future. They may be asked to draw a line representing key events using different colours and symbols. Alternatively, they could use a two-dimensional graph with time as the x axis and, say, self esteem or well-being as the y axis.
- Written portrayals may use questions such as 'What do you seem to seek out, or avoid, in your life?', 'What are your most satisfying achievements?' or 'What would you most like to be doing in ten years time?'

Card Sorts

A card sort is an activity in which an individual is given a set of cards and asked to sort them in some meaningful order. Each card usually represents something relating to career decision-making, for example, a skill or a work value (a satisfaction sought from work). Individuals may be asked to put the cards in rank order, according to its importance to them. Alternatively, clients may be required to sort them into various piles, for example, those that are very important, somewhat important or unimportant.

One example of a recently developed card sort is the Intelligent Career Card Sort (Parker, 2002). This is based on Arthur, Claman and DeFillipi's (1995) model of the 'intelligent career'. These authors suggested that career success and satisfaction depends on three 'career competencies' or 'career investments': 'knowing-why', 'knowing-how' and 'knowing-whom'. Knowing-why includes work values and the personal meaning of work, as well as work–life balance issues. Knowing-how reflects the skills and abilities of the individual, and includes both career-related and job-related skills and knowledge. Knowing-whom refers to the social contacts, attachments and relationships that the individual makes within and outside their organisation.

The card sort itself contains cards describing aspects of each type of career investment. Examples of 'knowing-why' are: 'I want to be challenged in my work', and 'I want to work in an industry that matters'. The 'knowing-how' cards include: 'I seek to apply the skills that I have' and 'I seek to become a better leader'. Examples of 'knowing-whom' are: 'I look for support from people who are interested in my career' and 'I work with people from whom I can learn'. Individuals are asked to select seven cards in each group that best describe their current career situation. They are then told to rank each set of seven in order of importance. One basic principle of the exercise is that each person interprets the cards in their own way, and therefore a discussion of the meaning of the selected cards is essential in the interpretation of results.

Like other tools, card sorts provide structure in dealing with a complex and unfamiliar task. Also, completing a card sort can be fun and engaging and therefore it can contribute much to developing the working alliance.

Checklists and Informal Rating Scales

These can be contrasted with standardised psychometric instruments. A simple checklist of aptitudes or interests, for example, may be helpful for clients who need a stimulus to discussion which can be administered fairly quickly. Many examples of these can be found in self-help materials and career planning workbooks. Hirsh and Jackson (1994), for example, have developed several simple tools for individuals to assess strengths, interests and values, and to compare options.

The types of tools and techniques described thus far in this chapter are often referred to as 'informal' instruments. Their advantages include: their low cost and flexibility; they often do not have to be ordered from a publisher; they may require less time to administer than more formal techniques; clients may feel less anxious completing them than with formal techniques, and have a greater sense of ownership of the results; and practitioners may not need lengthy training in their use.

However, several less positive characteristics of these tools should be noted. For example, standard ways of interpreting the results of these activities are rarely given, and therefore their interpretation is left entirely to the skill of the practitioner. Also the more quantitative methods, such as card sorts and check lists, rarely have known psychometric properties, such as reliability or validity, and they are rarely supported by data that allows individuals to compare their scores with other people.

The proliferation of these kinds of instruments suggests a lot of 'reinventing the wheel'. Keen to develop their own tools, practitioners and researchers rarely devote enough time to reviewing existing instruments and considering whether to use them intact or adapt them to suit their own needs.

Psychometric Tests and Inventories

Psychometric tests and inventories are commonly used in career counselling to assess not only attributes relevant to occupational choice, such as occupational interests, work values, aptitudes and personality, but also other components of career development, such as decision-making styles and skills, and career maturity (or psychological readiness for career development tasks). A database of British Psychological Society (BPS) recognised tests is available at www.psychtesting.org.uk, and this contains a list of those useful for counselling and career development. Many of these kinds of instruments are only available to individuals with appropriate training and experience. In the UK, for example, most tests and inventories are available only to those holding the BPS Level A or Level B qualification in occupational testing. (For more information about these qualifications, see Jackson (1996).) However, clients often come to career counselling with the results of tests administered in other settings, so it is important that career counsellors understand some of the basic principles of testing.

We will use the term 'tests' here to refer to measures that assess *maximum performance*. The underlying assumption of these is that individuals will attempt to perform at the top of their form. These instruments can be contrasted with measures of *typical response*, which are often called inventories. These are based on self-report, on individuals describing their likes and dislikes, or how they typically behave.

A distinction can also be made between instruments that help individuals assess the *content* of career choices, or 'what to choose', and those that assess the *process* of choice, or 'how to choose'. In general, the attributes described in Chapter 5 – strengths and weaknesses, personality traits, and interests and values – are important in considering the content of choice. Helping clients assess these characteristics enables them to explore characteristics that help them identify jobs or occupations to consider, following person–environment fit approaches.

Some career counselling clients also need help with assessing their decision-making skills, and instruments have been developed which assess these as well as career maturity (the individual's readiness for decision-making), career indecision, and other aspects of career choice processes. For example, if helping a client assess interests and abilities does not seem to enable them to move forward in their decision making, it may be helpful to try to identify any barriers or irrational beliefs that may be hindering progress. The Career Decision Scale (Osipow, Carney, Winer, Yanico & Koschier, 1997), described below, is one example of an instrument that identifies some of these attitudes and barriers.

Instruments assessing the content of career choices

Perhaps the most commonly used psychometric instruments used in career counselling are occupational interest inventories. Interest inventories are used mainly as an aid to self-assessment, helping individuals identify occupational fields that they are likely to enjoy working in. Typically, individuals' responses to the items in the inventory are compared to those of people working in a range of occupations, and the individual is then able to assess how similar their interests are to those of people working in those occupations. Some inventories provide the individual with a profile of scores on various dimensions of interests and compare the individual's profile with profiles of workers in certain occupations.

The Strong Interest Inventory

One of the most well-known interest inventories is the Strong Interest Inventory (Harmon, Hansen, Borgen & Hammer, 1994). It is based on Holland's (1997) model of occupational interests, and it uses both the above approaches in the interpretation of individuals' scores. Table 6.1 shows the categories of general occupational themes and basic interests used in this instrument.

The aim of using an interest inventory in career counselling is not to identify a specific occupation that suits the individual, but rather to help clients learn about potential jobs and how they differ. The lists of interests used in interest inventories also provide useful 'cognitive frameworks' of occupations for use in decision making.

Table 6.1   General occupational themes and basic interest scales used in the Strong Interest Inventory

General occupational themes	Basic interests scales
Realistic	Agriculture; Nature; Military activities; Athletics; Mechanical activities
Investigative	Science; Mathematics; Medical science
Artistic	Music/dramatics; Art; Applied arts; Writing; Culinary arts
Social	Teaching; Social services; Medical services; Religious activities
Enterprising	Public speaking; Law/politics; Merchandising; Sales; Organisational management
Conventional	Data management; Computer activities; Office services

The Minnesota Importance Questionnaire

Measures of work values, or basic beliefs about what is important to the individual in the work context, are also frequently used in career counselling. One example is the Minnesota Importance Questionnaire (Rounds, Henley, Dawis, Lofquist & Weiss, 1981). This instrument requires the individual to rate the importance of 20 work-related values or needs, each of which is represented by a statement. The 20 values, and the statements used to assess them, are as follows:

- Ability utilisation. I could do something that makes use of my abilities.
- Achievement. The job could give me a feeling of accomplishment.
- Activity. I could be busy all the time.
- Advancement. The job would provide an opportunity for advancement.
- Authority. I could tell people what to do.
- Company policies and practices. The company would administer its policies fairly.
- Compensation. My pay would compare well with that of other workers.
- Co-workers. My co-workers would be easy to make friends with.
- Creativity. I could try out some of my own ideas.
- Independence. I could work alone on the job.
- Moral values. I could do the work without feeling that it is morally wrong.
- Recognition. I could get recognition for the job I do.
- Responsibility. I could make decisions on my own.
- Security. The job would provide for steady employment.
- Social service. I could do things for other people.
- Social status. I could be 'somebody' in the community.
- Supervision-Human relations. My boss would back up the workers (with top management).
- Supervision-Technical. My boss would train the workers well.
- Variety. I could do something different every day.
- Working conditions. The job would have good working conditions.

Measures of ability are less often used in career counselling. However, some clients need help to assess whether they already possess, or could acquire, the abilities and skills required to do a particular job. Tests of both general ability and specific aptitudes may be used in this context. A measure of ability that is widely used in the UK is the Watson-Glaser Critical Thinking Appraisal (Watson & Glaser, 1994). This requires the individual to read passages and answer questions on it. The test assesses the ability to make inferences, recognise assumptions, make deductions, interpret data, and evaluate arguments.

Personality measures may be used to help individuals assess their personal style of relating to people and understanding one's personality can also help in choosing a suitable occupational setting as well as a particular occupation. Commonly used measures include Cattell's 16PF (Cattell, Eber & Tatsuoka, 1970), the Occupational Personality Questionnaire (Saville, Holdsworth, Nyfield, Cramp & Mabey, 1984), and the Myers-Briggs Type Indicator (Myers & McCaulley, 1985). Instruments based on the 'Big Five' model of personality (e.g. Costa & McCrae, 1992), outlined in Chapter 1, are less frequently used.

The 16PF
The 16PF assesses the following dimensions of personality:

- Reserved: outgoing
- More intelligent: less intelligent
- Emotional: calm
- Humble: assertive
- Serious: happy-go-lucky
- Expedient: conscientious
- Shy: uninhibited
- Tough-minded: tender-minded
- Trusting: suspicious
- Practical: imaginative
- Forthright: calculating
- Self assured: apprehensive
- Conservative: radical
- Group membership: self-sufficiency
- Undisciplined: controlled
- Relaxed: tense

Apart from interests, values, abilities and personality, writers are increasingly noting the so-called 'soft skills' necessary for surviving in changing work environments. Chartrand and Walsh (2001), for example, argue that certain interpersonal skills and cognitive style characteristics (for example, creativity and effective problem solving) are increasingly important. 'Emotional intelligence' (Salovey & Mayer, 1990) has also been emphasised: this includes abilities such as self-control, persistence and ability to judge the emotions of others. Psychologists have been devoting a considerable amount of effort into developing instruments to measure these constructs, but as yet they are little used in career counselling.

Instruments assessing career choice processes

These instruments focus on the assessment of the kinds of skills needed for effective decision making and the problems and processes of career decision making. New instruments are frequently emerging, but most concentrate on the assessment of career maturity, career indecision and uncertainty, and barriers to making a career choice. A good summary of some existing instruments can be found in Niles and Harris-Bowlsbey (2002). Here we will focus on two types of measures: career maturity and career indecision.

In the United States, a lot of attention has been given to the assessment of the personal qualities that help prepare the individual for career decision making. As we saw in Chapter 2, Super and Overstreet (1960) proposed the term 'career maturity' to describe the coping behaviours needed to deal with career tasks. At the stage of early exploration, career maturity was defined as the individual's readiness for career decision making. Drawing on developmental psychology, a list of the characteristics and behaviours which might constitute vocational maturity in adolescence was constructed.

Later models and measures drew on this work, and since then several measures of career maturity have been developed. Two examples are the Career Maturity Inventory and the Career Development Inventory.

The Career Maturity Inventory (CMI)

Crites' (1978) Career Maturity Inventory has two sections: the Competence Test and the Attitude Scale. The Competence Test is designed to assess the degree to which individuals possess the career information, planning and decision making skills to make realistic and wise decisions. There are five sub-scales:

- Self-appraisal – knowing yourself.
- Occupational information – knowing about jobs.
- Goal selection – choosing a job.
- Planning – looking ahead.
- Problem solving – what should they do?

The Attitude Scale measures individuals' maturity of attitudes towards careers and career choices. Again there are five sub-scales, measuring the following attitudes towards decision making:

- Decisiveness – extent to which individual is definite about making a career choice.
- Involvement – extent to which individual is actively participating in the process of making a choice.
- Independence – extent to which individual relies on others in the occupational choice.
- Orientation – task or pleasure orientation in attitudes towards work.
- Compromise – extent to which individual is willing to compromise between needs and reality.

The Career Development Inventory (CDI)

The Career Development Inventory (Super et al., 1981) is designed to assess similar attributes. The sub-scales are as follows:

- Career planning
- Career exploration
- Decision making
- World of work information
- Knowledge of preferred occupational group

Both the CMI and the CDI are used for diagnostic purposes in individual career counselling, to assess areas where clients may need particular support. They are also used in the evaluation of career interventions, and as we saw in Chapter 4, career counselling has been found to affect positively career maturity as measured by these instruments.

'Indecision' in career choice refers to the inability of individuals to commit themselves to a career direction. One example of an instrument designed to measure indecision is the Career Decision Scale (Osipow et al., 1997).

The Career Decision Scale

The first two items of this scale ask the individual to indicate whether or not he or she has made a definite choice of educational course and career. The aggregate score is an index of vocational/educational uncertainty.

The remaining items assess various possible causes of career indecision. These are organised into four factors:

- Lack of structure and confidence – lacking a clear self identity.
- Approach-approach conflict – difficulty in deciding between several options.
- External barriers – constraints to choice arising from factors outside the individual.
- Personal conflict – going against the wishes of someone else.

Again, this measure has been used both in individual diagnosis and evaluation.

Judging tests and inventories

Clearly, psychological tests and inventories should produce accurate measurements of the constructs they assess. They should therefore possess adequate *reliability*. The reliability coefficient of an instrument indicates the extent to which it is stable, or capable of producing consistent results. An instrument should also be *valid*, measuring what it aims to measure.

Published tests and inventories often permit comparisons to be made with other people, using norms from an appropriate criterion group. Raw scores obtained directly from a measure are often meaningless unless considered in relation to the performance of a specific group of individuals. However, the norms used to interpret a given score depend on the client and the purpose for which the assessment is being carried out.

Fairness is also important, and the practitioner needs to know which populations have been used to test and standardise the instrument. Gender, ethnic background, age and types of disability will all be relevant. Space precludes discussing these issues in depth, and there are many texts on testing which provide a thorough analysis of psychometrics. A good introduction is provided by Jackson (1996).

Using assessment tools in career counselling

The results of assessment tools are generally seen as just one of the elements in helping. As the developmental orientation to career counselling suggests, the client should be involved in the selection of tools, and as an equal partner, not a passive recipient of knowledge. Clients should be adequately prepared for the assessment process; this may include explaining what they will get out of the assessment; explaining the activity and how long it will take to complete it, telling them when the results will be available (if there will be a delay); explaining how the results will be reported, and being clear what will happen to the results.

Nathan and Hill (2006) emphasise the importance of giving clients space to discuss their response to completing an exercise or instrument. In this excerpt from a career counselling session, they show how talking through reactions to an exercise led to a useful discussion of strengths, even before the content of the exercises were discussed:

Dave:	I haven't had the time to do all these exercises.
Career counsellor (Cc):	You've been really busy then.
Dave:	Yes, and I just couldn't think how to start.
Cc:	So the questions were hard?
Dave:	No ... I mean yes ... well I don't think I've ever achieved anything.
Cc:	Yes, 'achievement' is a strong word.
Dave:	Hmm ... well there *have* been some good times.
Cc:	Can I hear about one of them? (Nathan & Hill, 2006: 80)

In addition, practitioners have an ethical responsibility to move beyond the straightforward interpretation of assessments to helping clients to use the results in managing their careers. This involves a shift from presenting data to making inferences about the meaning of the data. When using instruments that relate individual attributes to occupations, it is useful to:

- Consider the attributes measured by the instrument and check with the client on their accuracy.
- Check with the client as to whether some attributes are over- or under-emphasised in the total picture.
- Discuss with the client whether some information from the assessment is only relevant to certain stages or a passing stage in development.
- Check whether some information has been overlooked because it does not fit neatly with the rest.
- Discuss with the client how far the information takes account of the desired or future self as well as the present self.
- Help the client to think broadly about how the combination of characteristics relate to a broad range of occupations.

- Help the client to consider the lifestyle implications of the occupations identified by an instrument, including travel, income and working hours.
- Suggest ways to explore occupational options when they have been identified, for example, job shadowing, viewing videos, internships and part-time work.
- After some of this exploration has been carried out, offer a follow-up interview to help them evaluate what they have learned, and to decide whether to keep specific occupations on a short list or discard them.

Summary

A range of tools and techniques can be used for assessment in career counselling and we have discussed some examples of these in this chapter. They include systematic reflection on experience; graphic and written portrayals; card sorts; checklists and informal rating scales; and psychometric tests and inventories. In our discussion of psychometric instruments, two groups of measures were identified: those assessing the content of choices, and those assessing career choice processes. Psychometric instruments need to demonstrate adequate reliability and validity, and norms should be derived from an appropriate criterion group. Most writers emphasise the importance of involving clients in the selection of assessment tools, preparing them for the assessment process, giving them opportunities to discuss their reactions to completing an instrument, and help them consider the meaning of the results for their career development.

Discuss and Debate

1   In this chapter, we have looked at the assessment of occupational interests, work values, abilities and personality. What other attributes relating to the content of choices might be assessed in career counselling?
2   In what situations might it be useful to use instruments that assess the process of career choice?
3   What are the advantages and disadvantages of using informal exercises and checklists in career counselling, as compared with psychometric tests and inventories?

SEVEN   Career Information

This chapter begins by discussing clients' differing needs for information and its purposes. Then we discuss various ways of describing work, including the adequacy of current constructs and frameworks in use in the UK, and how different frameworks may have different kinds of uses. It may seem a little strange to be asked to think about the *nature* of the frameworks we use, but the world of work is changing in many ways, and traditional ways of describing work may not now be so appropriate. In the last section of the chapter we consider some aspects of the career counsellor's role in relation to career information.

Clients' Needs for Information

Clearly, different client groups will need different kinds of career information. This will depend on their age, life stage and level of qualifications, among other things. For example, young people in the early stages of thinking about careers may value broad frameworks which portray clusters of occupations and differences between them, those returning to employment after a career break may need to analyse opportunities in terms of transferable skills, and those in mid-career may need highly specific occupational and educational information.

Information needs will also differ according to the type of decision being made. Clients may be facing a wide variety of different types of career moves, including initial occupational choices, educational choices, changes in occupation, choice of employers, changes in contractual state, or intraorganisational moves. Also, geographical considerations will vary: some clients will need detailed information about local labour markets, while for others national data will be required.

Offer (2001) has suggested that the questions most commonly asked by clients about career opportunities are in the areas of:

- Demand for labour. This covers questions to do with how competitive entry into a particular job or field tends to be.
- Progression routes, career structure and earnings. This involves questions concerning general prospects, including lateral mobility and opportunities for promotion.
- Geographical availability. This involves the availability of appropriate opportunities within the client's normal travel-to-work area.

- Trends. Questions here concern whether opportunities are increasing or decreasing in a particular field.
- Transferability. This covers issues concerning how far skills developed in one occupation or sector are transferable to another.
- Recruitment and selection methods. Issues here concern where vacancies are advertised, how to apply and what selection processes are used.

However, it would be impossible for a career counsellor to have all the answers to these different types of questions at their fingertips. What is more important is to know where to find the answers, or where to advise clients to begin their research. Career information is available widely via all kinds of media, for example, the internet, newspapers, professional journals and publications, videos and DVDs. A useful list of UK information sources is provided in Nathan and Hill (2006).

Career counsellors do have several specific responsibilities relating to career information, though, as Niles and Harris-Bowlsbey (2002) suggest. First, the materials they direct clients to (printed materials, computer-based systems, or websites) should be high in quality. For example, data should be updated regularly, and the vocabulary should be appropriate for those reading it. It should also be accurate and free from bias against those with disabilities, or bias based on gender, ethnicity or age.

Secondly, career counsellors have a responsibility to make the availability of resources known to their clients, acquaint clients with them, and refer them to the specific resources that may be particularly helpful to them.

The third responsibility is to help the client process the information or data. Niles and Harris-Bowlsbey (2002) suggest that the practitioner should have the following concerns:

- Is this client ready to receive data and deal with it effectively?
- What barriers does the client potentially have to using data effectively?
- What kinds of data, and how much, will be most helpful?
- What methods of receiving data – print material, computers and websites, personal contact – will be most effective?
- What kind of decision style does the client use, and how will that affect his or her ability to use data effectively? (Niles & Harris-Bowlsbey, 2002: 184)

Not all clients need career information. A presenting need for information could mask other concerns, and these may only become apparent some way into the career counselling process. Also, responding directly to a simple request for information may serve to confuse the client rather than help them. As Gysbers et al. (2003) argue, the essence of effective career counselling is knowing whether, when and how to provide information.

Take, for example, a recent graduate who comes for counselling because he is disappointed with the unchallenging nature of his first job, and asks for information about what else he can do with a degree in librarianship. It would be important to explore why he is dissatisfied rather than immediately respond to the request for information. In general, it is difficult to assess clients' needs for information before we have enough information about their situation.

Purposes of Information

Useful distinctions between the various purposes of providing information have been offered by Gysbers et al. (2003). Purposes can be either educational or motivational.

For educational purposes, information may inform thinking, expand and extend it, or correct it. Informing and expanding may often be fairly straightforward processes, whilst correcting it may be more problematic, as the individual may have held on to distorted information for some time. For example, a client may be under the misapprehension that all jobs in financial services require a high degree of mathematical ability, which she feels she does not have. In holding on to that information she is restricting her options. Correcting this misapprehension would involve giving her quite detailed information about the range of jobs in this sector and the skills involved.

For motivational purposes, information can be used to stimulate clients to seek more information, or challenge or confirm what they already know. Gysbers et al. (2003) argue that when provided at the right moment, information can make all the difference in career planning. Stimulating and challenging need to be carried out at 'teachable moments', when the information will encourage the client to explore more deeply. Confirming the information that clients already have can be reassuring and this too can allow clients to move forward.

Types of Career Information

In career counselling a variety of frameworks and constructs are used to describe the world of work and to help individuals relate themselves to it. Hirsh, Kidd and Watts (1998) have identified several types of constructs and frameworks currently in use in the UK, including:

- Employment constructs, which are used to describe jobs, occupations, sectors and contractual modes of employment.
- Employers' constructs, which differentiate within the organisation between jobs.
- Classifications linking individual characteristics to opportunities, for example, interests, values, abilities and skills.
- Skills, competences and qualifications, which are used to describe the requirements of work.

Multidimensional frameworks, which combine aspects of other classifications, are also used.

Employment constructs

Occupations

An occupation describes a group of similar jobs across organisations. In the UK the Standard Occupational Classification (SOC) is used as the standard system for almost all employment-related data. This identifies and groups occupations by similarity of qualifications, training, skills and experience. At the most general level, occupations are placed into nine 'major groups': managers and administrators; professional; associate professional and technical; clerical and secretarial; craft and related; personal and protective services; sales; plant and machine operatives; and other. Table 7.1 shows the nine major groups and some examples of the minor groups they contain.

SOC is used as the standard system in the UK for the collection of almost all employment-related data. However, it has several limitations.

Table 7.1   Examples of Standard Occupational Classification groups

Major groups	Minor group examples
1 Managers and administrators	Specialist managers; Managers in transport and storing; Protection service officers
2 Professional occupations	Natural scientists; Engineers and technologists; Health professionals
3 Associate professional and technical occupations	Scientific technicians; Draughtspersons, quantity and other surveyors; Literary, artistic and sports professionals
4 Clerical and secretarial occupations	Filing and records clerks; Secretaries, personal assistants, typists, word processor operators
5 Craft and related occupations	Construction trades, Printing and related trades; Woodworking trades
6 Personal and protective services	Catering occupations; Health and related occupations
7 Sales occupations	Buyers, brokers and related agents; Sales representatives; Sales assistants and check-out operators
8 Plant and machine operatives	Textiles and tannery process operatives; Assemblers/line workers; Road transport operatives
9 Other occupations	Other occupations in mining and manufacturing; Other occupations in sales and services

Source: Hirsh et al. (1998: 5)

Because of changes in the labour market, the descriptions have become out of date and some SOC groupings have become unwieldy and not detailed enough. There are also conceptual difficulties with SOC as some groupings focus more on level of work and others on sector.

Sectors

The Standard Industrial Classification (SIC) is used in the UK to classify sectors of employment. At the most general level, nine main sectors are used: agriculture and fishing; energy and water; manufacturing; construction; distribution, hotels and restaurants; transport and communications; banking, finance and insurance; public administration, education and health; other services.

Providing clients with information about employment sectors can be helpful because it may link to individuals' knowledge of employers, and there are strong similarities within sectors in the kinds of work on offer. Sectors also have some common elements of culture and work patterns. Also, many employment forecasts describe opportunities by employment sector. However, some occupations are found across nearly all sectors.

Contracts

Employment information is also collected and presented to show contractual differences (eg full-time/part-time, temporary/permanent). For some individuals (e.g. parents looking for part-time employment) labour market information on where such work is available is essential, and it may determine their occupational choice.

Employers' constructs

Job descriptions and job titles

Traditionally, employers advertised opportunities using job descriptions. Job titles are still used in external recruitment, but they are now frequently supplemented by descriptions of skills, personal attributes or experience, and the qualifications required by applicants. Job titles are still used internally, too, but these are sometimes inadequate descriptors of job content.

Hirsh et al. (1998) suggest that new frameworks seem to be emerging in employing organisations. These include broad levels of work, job families (groups of jobs with similar skills and areas of knowledge), descriptions of broad work roles, and skill and competence frameworks.

Classifications linking individual characteristics to opportunities

We discussed the individual attributes relevant to career development and career counselling in Chapters 5 and 6. Many of these attributes have been deliberately developed to help individuals relate themselves to opportunities, and the same terms are often used to describe both individuals and work environments. These include frameworks of interests, values and skills.

Interests

As we saw earlier, occupational interests refer to a person's preferences for particular work activities. One of the best-known interest frameworks is Holland's RIASEC model (Holland, 1997), which sets out six interest types: realistic, investigative, artistic, social, enterprising and conventional. (These types were described in Chapter 1.)

However, interests described at a more detailed level may be more useful than these kinds of categories (for example, writing and teaching). These kinds of labels may be more in line with the language individuals use themselves to describe their interests. It could be argued though that the more general, underlying dimensions are also helpful in broadening individuals' perspectives by linking preferred activities to others which are similar. Interest frameworks in general can also be criticised for not taking enough account of emerging work roles which may demand a wider range of interests.

Values

Frameworks of values describe the satisfactions sought in work and educational environments. Relatively few of these types of frameworks exist to describe work, however, and this is perhaps because it is possible to satisfy particular values in a range of different contexts. In the UK, Career Builder, a computer-aided guidance system, attempts a classification of values in relation to occupations, as does Prospects Planner, another computer-aided system (outlined in Chapter 8).

There are similarities between systems of work values and Schein's (1993) career anchor framework, but in some ways the latter is conceptually broader. According to Schein, career anchors consist of a mix of needs, values and skills which, as 'evolving themes' in career development, wed people to particular work roles. These are:

- Security/stability
- Autonomy/independence
- Technical or functional competence
- General managerial competence
- Entrepreneurial activity
- Service/dedication to a cause
- Pure challenge
- Life-style integration

Because of its developmental emphasis this framework may be most useful in career counselling in mid-career and in analyses of organisational environments.

Skills

Frameworks based on individuals' abilities and skills are commonly used in computer-aided guidance systems and other self-assessment tools to match individual characteristics (usually self-reported) to opportunities. Many frameworks exist, often based on long-standing psychological models of individual aptitudes and abilities. For example, one UK university careers service uses a framework describing skills in ten areas: working creatively; handling numerical data; working with text; practical competence; problem solving; organising; carrying out research; relating to people; influencing; communicating.

Many career practitioners in the UK use the Morrisby Profile, which assesses aptitudes together with aspects of personality, work style and interests and provides occupational suggestions based on the interrelationship of scores on each dimension. The framework of transferable skills employed in the Headway computer-aided guidance system allows assessments based on skills developed in home making or leisure activities. As with interests, it is becoming increasingly common for career counsellors to develop their own skills frameworks to suit their needs.

In addition to describing individuals' characteristics, skills are also used to describe the requirements of work. As jobs change and become more flexible, skills may become a more reliable construct on which to base descriptions of work. Since skills belong to individuals as well as being required by jobs, they potentially form a useful bridging construct in career counselling between individual characteristics and work opportunities. Skills also take account of knowledge gained through experience and training, and so they are useful in describing career progression.

Competences ('es') are behavioural descriptions of desired aspects of work performance (for example, 'communicates well with customers'). In the UK, National Vocational Qualifications (NVQs) and Scottish Vocational Qualifications (SVQs) use this notion of competence. Competencies ('ies') are behaviours deriving from underlying personal characteristics (for example, cognitive abilities) and these are much used by employers, particularly in selection and development.

Although skills are useful in descriptions of work, they have not often been used to classify work. Because each job requires so many skills and to different degrees, skill frameworks may be more useful as descriptive material about jobs than as a classification system *per se*. Also a lot of emphasis has been placed on core skills, which are common across jobs and rarely differentiate between them.

Using Constructs of Work in Career Counselling

Hirsh et al. (1998) argue that these various frameworks can help individuals in developing conceptual tools which help them identify and sift information relevant to them. However, the constructs and frameworks used to describe work mainly focus on choice of occupation, and on interests and values. Not all clients need occupational information: many will be more concerned with information that helps them with decisions relating to other aspects of working life (for example, choice of type of organisation or employer, or decisions about whether to work full- or part-time).

Another drawback with many frameworks is that they are largely static, they do not take enough account of how careers develop over time. People are increasingly following career patterns which comprise jobs requiring similar skills and knowledge that are easy to move between, and so showing how a particular type of work experience enables individuals to move to another kind of work is now more important. However, descriptions of careers in these terms need to be updated regularly as career paths and labour markets change.

Hirsh et al. (1998) also suggest that because the language of skills can describe progression and development, there is a strong argument for skills replacing occupations as the dominant construct for highlighting similarities and differences between types of work. However, there are no well-developed frameworks for skills that are widely accepted in the UK, and it seems likely that skill information is better seen as illustrative and descriptive rather than a potentially exhaustive classification system.

Career Information Within the System of Opportunities

So far, in our discussion of the role of information in career counselling, we have assumed that the main task of the career counsellor in relation to the labour market is to help clients access career information and relate it to themselves. But it has been argued that career practitioners might also work beyond the level of the individual, to work for social change (Watts, 1996a). They might challenge the system that relegates some people to poorly paid, unskilled work, perhaps by working within local communities to expose issues of social justice and inform institutional and national policies (see, for example, Irving, 2005).

Although some see these radical objectives as unrealistic and inappropriate (e.g. Roberts, 2005), there is a strong case for improving the individual help given to people destined for work in the secondary sector (jobs with poor conditions, insecurity, low pay, little training and few prospects). Large numbers of people work in this sector, particularly in developing countries, and their information needs are wide ranging. Many will need advice about employment rights, welfare benefits, and trade unions, and, arguably, support in influencing the social and political structures that produce these jobs (Offer, 2001).

Summary

Clients have varied needs for information, and the purposes of providing it will accordingly differ. Information can inform, expand and extend knowledge, correct misapprehensions, stimulate more information seeking, challenge the client to think more deeply or confirm the knowledge that the client already has. Career counsellors use a range of work-related frameworks and constructs, depending on clients' needs. These include employment constructs, employers' constructs, classifications linking individuals to opportunities and frameworks of skills, competences and qualifications. Less attention has been given in the literature to the information needed by those working in the secondary sector, but many will need a broader range of information than is usually provided.

Discuss and Debate

1 Think back to a time when you were making an important decision about your career or an educational opportunity. What kind of career information did you need at the time? How might this information be accessed?

2 If you are an employee, describe the job descriptions and job titles used in your organisation. How useful are they in communicating the nature of jobs to other people both inside and outside the organisation?

3 If you wanted to carry out some research into how various constructs and frameworks of work are used in career counselling, what research questions would you want to address?

4 How far should career counsellors work to promote social change as well as individual change?

EIGHT   Using Information and Communications Technology in Career Counselling

In this chapter we discuss how information and communications technology (ICT) has been used in career counselling. We begin by outlining some of the computer-aided guidance systems (CAGS) that have been developed over the years. We then discuss the use of the internet in career counselling.

Computer-aided Guidance Systems

A computer-aided guidance system is a set of activities, delivered by a computer, which has been developed to assist with career planning. CAGS have various functions in career counselling. Offer (1997) has classified the systems into eight categories:

- Self assessment – programs that help individuals assess themselves and which provide a profile in terms that also describe work or educational opportunities. These are commonly based on occupational interests.
- Matching systems – programs that match individuals to occupations or courses. These are the most commonly used applications of computers in career counselling.
- Information retrieval – databases of education and training opportunities, or of employers.
- Games and simulations – business, training or other career education materials. These enable users to explore occupations in an experiential way.
- Decision aids – programs that help individuals analyse the factors they use in decision making, and apply these to a typical decision.
- Dedicated word processors – programs that provide support for CV writing or completing application forms.
- Computer-based training – programs that teach job-seeking skills, for example, handling interviews and making job applications.
- Psychometric tests – programs that administer psychological tests and inventories. These are mainly online adaptations of pencil-and-paper tests, measuring abilities, aptitudes, personality etc.

Some systems – 'mini systems' – just cover one or two of these functions. Others – 'maxi systems' – address most of the functions in an integrated way which enables users to move flexibly between tasks. As well as being practically more convenient to use, maxi systems model a career decision-making process. Users therefore acquire not only information, but also skills and frameworks which they can apply to current and future career decisions.

One UK example of a maxi system is Prospects Planner. This is a CAGS designed specifically for use in higher education. It comprises self-assessment of abilities, interests and values; comparison of self with career options; occupational information; and advice on the tactics of making job applications. Over 400 profiles of graduate occupations are covered, including information about work activities; entry requirements; availability of jobs; age barriers/gender balance; life style implications/salaries; and possible career development.

The theoretical bases of different CAGS vary. Some, for example, take a person–environment fit perspective, matching individual objectively assessed attributes to opportunities in an 'expert' way. Others work in a phenomenological way with the individual's own constructs of decision making, assuming that this represents the way in which individuals actually construct their own reality.

Using CAGS in career counselling

Watts (1996b) notes that in many respects computer-aided guidance systems simulate a career counselling session. This is because, in principle, the computer can deliver any pre-designed interview sequence that the system developer wants to offer. Career counsellors, however, can respond intuitively and flexibly to any given situation. In the case of computer systems, any such flexibility has to be consciously built into the system itself, using principles which are potentially transparent and open to inspection.

CAGS offer an impressive range of capabilities related to helping people with career planning. They can store, update and retrieve large quantities of information; they can 'converse' with users, helping them clarify their needs; they can collate needs; and they can search, assemble and edit data that meets these needs (Watts, 1996b).

More specifically, they can reliably administer tests and inventories and score them. The user can be provided with a detailed report, which might include graphics that help to explain the meaning of the report. In addition, they can deliver the same service to users from any location, providing assistance in a standard way. If a record is kept in the computer for each user, the content can be customised for each person, depending on the results of past usage, or identified needs. CAGS can also search large databases of occupational and educational opportunities, if necessary combining search characteristics. These databases can be updated quickly, particularly if they are connected to an internet site that maintains them.

Computers are also capable of what Niles and Harris-Bowlsbey (2002) call 'crosswalking', meaning that they can easily relate one database to another. For example, the user may be able to crosswalk from a database of degree subjects to a database of subjects related to particular occupations. Links may also be provided from the CAGS to websites that can provide further information.

CAGS also have the potential to monitor the progress of the user through the process, and report progress to a third party. This provides an opportunity to link career counselling services to the user. Providing instruction is also a feature of some CAGS. This may include information on how occupations are organised, how to write a CV, or tips on job interviews.

Computers are therefore a potentially powerful resource to improve the quality of career counselling. However, as Watts (1996b) points out, computers can be seen as reducing knowledge, wisdom and experience to data and they can be used to mechanise the human interaction which is seen as so central to career counselling. They also manipulate these data according to strict logic. This means that the more affective and personal aspects of career development and career decision making cannot be adequately addressed by a computer. Even the best applications of artificial intelligence can only *mimic* the core conditions of the counselling relationship.

Watts (1996b) sees the challenge for career guidance services as being able to utilise computer technology in ways which supplement the potential of the practitioner, rather than restrict or replace it. Indeed, as we shall see later, research suggests that computer-aided guidance systems are more effective when used in conjunction with career counselling (Whiston et al., 2003). This is probably because career counsellors have an important role in providing support to clients using CAGS. For example, they can assess the readiness of the client to use the system; expand on the results of psychometric tests and inventories; motivate and support the client for continued career exploration; and suggest creative options that have not been offered by the system (Niles & Harris-Bowlsbey, 2002).

There are various ways in which computer-aided guidance systems can be incorporated into career counselling. For example, the client can be seen immediately before and/or after using the system. Or systems can be incorporated within the career counselling session, so that the client and the counsellor can work on the system together. But computer-aided guidance systems are also frequently used on a 'standalone' basis, in isolation from other guidance activities. Some clients may prefer to use systems in this way. And the burgeoning number of websites that offer help with career decision making suggests that many individuals find using the internet, without the support of a guidance practitioner, helpful in career planning. This brings us to the next topic of this chapter: the use of the internet.

The Internet in Career Counselling

Many CAGS offer a parallel version accessible via the internet. As a medium for delivery, the internet has several advantages over a stand alone or networked computer. First, it is available 24 hours a day to those who have access. Secondly, databases can be updated more frequently from one central source.

A third advantage is that links to other internet resources can be easily incorporated. This is particularly important in helping clients learn from the process of career exploration. One of the key tasks of career counselling, particularly within stages 3 and 4 of the process – exploring new perspectives, and forming strategies and plans – is the shift back and forth between *focus* and *scope*, to use Bedford's (1982) terminology. Offer (2000) has suggested that another way of describing this is as a cycle of loosening and tightening. First the concern may be to open up possibilities and to break down rigidities of thinking. Later, a tightening of ideas may be necessary, with a sharper discrimination between options. Offer argues that the structure of the web, with its hyperlinked network of connections, mirrors the process of loosening and tightening. Ideas can be loosened and linked to other ideas. When users click on a word or image that stands out from the text (both literally and metaphorically), they are led into another extension of the system of constructs used, and possibly of their own construct system also.

Offer (2000) gives an example of clicking on the key word 'Modern Apprenticeship'. (In the early 2000s this term was used for apprenticeship schemes in the UK.)

The link may be a lateral link – the data that lies behind the hypertext link could be an alternative set of ideas at the same level of importance. If the key word is 'Modern Apprenticeship' it could lead to a definition of the term, or, more interestingly, an account of National Traineeships, GNVQ, or A levels as an alternative. Such hyperlinks would constantly expand your ideas. This, interestingly, is seldom done, but it could serve a clear guidance function – widening scope, ensuring you haven't missed alternatives, loosening ideas, freeing up the imagination … . On the other hand, it may be a vertical link: one that takes you up the ladder, so to speak, to ideas and concepts that subsume this text or image as part of their domain, or down the ladder to an example of what this text, word, or this image contains within its own domain of meaning. In the case of 'Modern Apprenticeship' the hyperlink could lead *down* to a case study of an individual apprentice or a list of available programmes or companies offering them. It might also lead *up* to a statement of its advantages and disadvantages, with reasons why you should or should not undertake such an option, or, at an even more superordinate level, to a discussion of the idea and value of training for a job – of which the apprenticeship is just one example. (Offer, 2000: 61–2)

This point is important because we need to understand the ways in which resources in general, and technology in particular, map onto existing theories and practice. The internet helps in elaborating ideas and this is one of the central activities in career counselling. Offer (2000) argues that if we become more conscious of how people expand and elaborate ideas we can design better websites and use existing ones more effectively.

In addition to formal CAGS, there are hundreds, if not thousands, of websites that are potentially helpful in career decision making and career management. One of the main search engines (e.g. www. google.com) can be used to search for sites by entering various key terms (for example, 'career decision making' or 'career planning'). These websites vary considerably in their aims. Some address the same sorts of functions that computer-aided guidance systems address, for example, self-assessment and information retrieval. Others help users exchange experiences with others in a similar situation, or give access to experts who can offer advice on different topics. A huge online labour market is now also developing.

Some websites signpost other sites where you will be likely to find the resources or information to meet your needs. These gateway sites are sometimes called 'portals'. Using these is often quicker than using a search engine, and it is more likely that what you find will be relevant. As Offer (2000) points out, a gateway site also offers a structure for making sense of career-related information. It can also help clients identify their own needs, prompting them to think more deeply about what they are looking for.

Evaluating websites

How can we judge the value of websites in the context of career counselling and career planning? With regard to what one might expect from a site, Offer (2000) suggests a range of questions, some interconnected, that can be used in judging its quality.

- Who produced this? What's in it for them? Could there be a conflict of interest? If so, is that openly acknowledged and declared?
- Can I trust them? What are their credentials? Are they relevant to the matter in hand? How else can I contact them if I need to? (or, Why have they not allowed me to do so?)
- Is it up to date? (And how do I tell?) When was it created and when was it last amended? What does it tell me? (What did I want to know that isn't here? What could they have told me that isn't here? Why didn't they?)
- Is it credible? (If not entirely, why should I believe this over another source that says something different?) Does it fit with what I already know about this subject?
- Can it be corroborated? (Where else can I get information about this? How valid and reliable would that be – more than this?) Does the site itself

offer relevant sources and indications as to where its statements can be checked?

- What signs are there, if any, of a lack of quality control on this site? (Any signs of sloppy thinking or practice, even simple misspellings?)
- Who is this aimed at/intended for? Is the agenda persuasion, or a balanced summary of the arguments or available facts? Does it acknowledge any alternative views?
- What other sites does it link to, or what other sources does it suggest – and does that indicate anything about the standpoint of this one?
- What other sources of this information, advice or guidance are there and how might they help me? Would they be better for my purposes than what is offered here? (Offer, 2000: 40)

Challenges for career counsellors

Although ICT has revolutionised career counselling, there are several concerns that practitioners need to address. First, not everyone has access to the internet, and younger people tend to be more active users than older people. If we want to ensure equitable access to the internet we will have to attend to individuals' physical access to the technology and how affordable this is, and people's confidence in using computers.

Secondly, as Offer (2000) points out, the user may come to career counselling better informed about some aspects of the issues that concern them than the career counsellor. Just as doctors now see more 'expert patients', so clients may have large amounts of detailed knowledge about opportunities. Many career counsellors will welcome this, because their sessions with the client can then deal with in-depth issues that require face-to-face discussion, not straightforward information giving. However, the lack of control over information on the internet means that users will often be gathering partial, out-of-date or false information. Arguably, therefore, the career counselling process may need to include the educative function of equipping users to be more critical and demanding of websites.

Thirdly, guidance practitioners and clients should beware of false optimism about the potential of web-based career assessment tools. Few come with appropriate caveats, and users are rarely helped to assess critically their psychometric qualities. The purpose of a tool, its development, psychometric characteristics, applicability and limitations should be presented clearly to users, but this information is often lacking. Oliver and Zack (1999) surveyed 24 free, internet-based self-assessment tools, rating each site against guidelines developed by the US National Career Development Association for career planning sites on the internet. They found that there was limited information about the site developers, limited evidence of test validity, and limited confidentiality. There is evidence too that some individuals benefit more than others from self-assessment tools. Specifically, those with low career maturity, limited verbal ability, and low self-confidence and low motivation may have difficulty with them (Prince, Most & Silver, 2003; Sampson, Peterson, Reardon & Lenz, 2000). There is also a risk of cultural bias: completing a test or inventory not intended for people with a specific cultural background is likely to produce misleading results.

Lastly, it should be recognised that the internet is an insecure environment. Clients need to be informed about levels of security on websites and the limitations of confidentiality.

Summary

In this chapter we discussed the use of computer-aided guidance systems and the internet in career counselling. CAGS are of various types. Mini-systems have only a small number of functions, for example, self-assessment and matching, while maxi-systems cover a range of functions, and often model the career decision-making process. Similarly, career management websites differ widely in their aims. This rapidly developing area presents many challenges for career counsellors, for example, how to use technology in a way that enhances the career counselling process, rather than restricting or routinising it. Also, the proliferation of websites raises questions about quality, and how clients may be helped to assess the value of the sites they access.

Discuss and Debate

1 Search for career-related websites using one of the main search engines (e.g. Google), entering various key terms (e.g. 'career decision making' or 'career planning'). Were the sites useful? In what ways?

2 Find a website that you have never visited before, which seems to be relevant to career counselling or career planning. Drawing on Offer's ideas, make some notes about what you would expect from a site like this, and the questions you would ask to judge its quality.

3 Think back to the approaches to career counselling you were introduced to earlier. Make a list of the main approaches and the activities and tasks involved in each. Then, alongside each activity and task, note some ways in which the internet can be helpful and some of the potential dangers of using the internet in this way.

NINE   Ethical Issues

Shahara, a third-year British Muslim student studying business studies came to see a careers adviser at the university careers service, saying that her parents had told her to come. Her family were from Bengal. She said she hoped very much to become a journalist, and she had completed a test on the internet which showed that she had a strong aptitude for this. During the session, it became clear that Shahara's family expected her to train to be an accountant after she graduated, and were very much against her going into journalism. The career adviser administered an occupational interests inventory, which showed a flat profile of interests, indicating that Shahara had no clear occupational preferences.

The careers adviser had concerns about the quality of aptitude test that Shahara had completed, as it appeared to be no more than a brief self-assessment device. She offered her a further appointment to explore her career aspirations further and a meeting was arranged for the following week.

The following day, the careers adviser received a phone call from Shahara's father, asking to be told what advice had been given to his daughter. She explained that issues discussed in career counselling were confidential, and it was up to Shahara to tell the father what had been discussed, if she wished. Over the next few days, the careers adviser received several more angry and abusive phone calls, demanding that the careers adviser arrange interviews for Shahara with accountancy firms. These caused the careers adviser considerable distress, but little support was forthcoming from her colleagues.

There are several issues embedded in this case study and most of these bear upon the ethics of effective practice:

- The confidentiality of the career counselling process.
- How to work with clients whose families have strong feelings about appropriate careers (is Shahara the only client?).
- The broader issue of the values inherent in career counselling and what happens when the emphasis on individual autonomy conflicts with cultural values.
- The quality of the online test and the ethics of offering testing over the internet.

- Whether the occupational interests measure was appropriate for a person from this cultural background.
- The university's responsibility to provide support for staff.

As can be seen in this case, the issue of values is particularly important in multicultural career counselling, and clients need to be understood within their cultural context, not just from the point of view of individual psychology. Any attempt to influence Shahara's career plans would need to be sensitive to the values inherent in more collectivist cultures. Confidentiality is commonly a difficult issue also. Furthermore, this case raises questions about the ethics of other parties, for example, those offering online career assessment and employers of career counsellors. Should an employer provide access to regular supervision for career counsellors, for example, and should career counsellors be required to attend supervision sessions?

Career counsellors need to be aware of the ethical and moral assumptions and values that they bring to their work, and they have a responsibility to act in an ethical manner. As well as the issues raised in the case above, common ethical concerns in career counselling include: dual relationships, for example personal and business relationships with clients; the limits of confidentiality in respect of legal obligations, for instance where there is a legal obligation to report a crime; practitioner accountability, that is, the question of on whose behalf is the career counsellor working; and issues of referral. Ethical issues are complex matters, and the aim of this chapter is to heighten awareness of them.

Dual Relationships

Dual relationships in career counselling and therapeutic counselling occur when the practitioner is involved in another different relationship with the client. Apart from the obvious personal and business relationships, there are instances where potential conflicts are less apparent, for example, helping the child of a friend. Although many of the same potential dilemmas arise in both therapeutic and career counselling, some are unique to career counselling. For example, Niles and Harris-Bowlsbey (2002) describe a situation where a career counsellor's work with a client simply entails commenting on his CV. A few weeks later they meet at a social event and begin a social relationship. The question arises as to whether that relationship is subject to the same ethical scrutiny as a relationship that involved several sessions of intensive career counselling. Several different answers are possible.

Pope (1991) has identified several ways in which dual relationships conflict with effective therapeutic counselling. First, they make professional boundaries unclear and therefore compromise the professional nature of the relationship. Secondly, they bring about a conflict of interest, since it could be argued that no longer is the counsellor there solely for the client. Thirdly, the counsellor is unable to enter into a subsequent non-therapy relationship with the client on an equal footing because of the personal material disclosed.

Confidentiality

Issues of confidentiality frequently raise difficulties for career counsellors, and this is largely because confidentiality is such an important aspect of the counselling relationship. Client–counsellor relationships are based on trust, and clients need to feel that what they disclose to the counsellor will not be used in ways that harm them.

Holmes and Lindley (1991) provide a persuasive case for the maintenance of confidentiality in psychotherapy. They argue that the subject matter of psychotherapy involves fears, fantasies and feelings that clients often find extremely hard to acknowledge. The normal rules of social encounters are suspended and clients need to feel safe to regress to kinds of behaviour that would be inappropriate in other settings. This feeling of safety requires a strong understanding between therapist and client that what goes on is confidential.

However, to this writer's knowledge, no national professional associations for counsellors suggest that confidentiality should be absolute. This would mean that counsellors could not communicate information to others so as to prevent serious harm to their clients.

Bond (2000) has argued that good practice on confidentiality should be guided by three principles:

- Disclosures should be in the client's best interests.
- They should be carried out only on a 'need to know' basis (that is, the recipient's need to have information in order to act in the client's best interests).
- They should be consistent with the purpose for which the client originally conveyed the information.

The ethic of respect for client autonomy suggests that client consent should be a prime consideration in decisions about confidentiality. In negotiating the initial contract or establishing a working alliance career counsellors might be explicit about disclosing information to others with the consent of the client. However, there will still be circumstances in which counsellors will judge that information should be disclosed, without the client's consent. Professional codes of practice stress the importance of confidentiality, but tend not to require that it should be absolute.

Accountability

Throughout the career counselling process, the practitioner needs to be clear on whose behalf they are working. Career counsellors who work on their own in private practice are unlikely to feel the need to be accountable to anyone other than their clients and their supervisor, if they have one. In other contexts, however, practitioners will be generally accountable to their managers and funding bodies, for example, advisers working for public sector agencies will be accountable to multiple stakeholders, including their board of management, which is ultimately accountable to government. As Watts (1996c) has pointed out, though, practitioners working in the public sector consistently assert that their primary client must be the individual, rather than government, or, indeed, employers. There are practical reasons for this as well as ethical ones: for example, practitioners can only serve their secondary clients (e.g. employers or government) if they have the trust and confidence of the clients with whom they are working. This suggests that the clients' interests should be given precedence, whilst recognising the need to show funding bodies that resources are being well-used. Quality assurance procedures (for example, the 'Matrix standard', described later) will have a role in demonstrating evidence of this, as will process and outcome research into the effectiveness of the career counselling provided. (This research is discussed in depth in Chapter 4.)

In some settings, for example, where the career counsellor is being paid by the client's employer, other parties may feel that they have legitimate influence on how practitioners carry out their day-to-day work. In this context, Sugarman (1992) recommends that practitioners consider the following:

- Find out what objectives the organisation is attempting to achieve in providing the service.
- Identify any areas where the provision of the service benefits the organisation at the expense of the individual.
- Identify any areas where the organisation goes beyond its right to control aspects of the employee's behaviour.
- Discuss what is implied by the term 'confidentiality' and negotiate the conditions under which it will and will not be maintained.
- Discover whether the resources are sufficient to do more good than harm, and in what ways the resources might compromise the aims of the service.
- Develop a written policy concerning the provision of the service.

Referral

At any stage in career counselling it may be appropriate to refer the client to another agency. For example, the process of career counselling may have led the client to feel the need for therapeutic counselling to deal with a major emotional issue. Or the client may need specialist information that the career counsellor is unable to provide. Practitioners need to be clear about when referral is necessary, recognising the boundaries between career counselling and other forms of intervention, and recognising the limits of their expertise. The decision to refer needs to be made jointly.

Sources of Ethics

Ideas about counselling ethics draw on many areas of insight. Bond (2000) has discussed six sources of ethics in counselling. His focus is on therapeutic counselling, but his points are equally relevant to career counselling.

Personal ethics

One clear source of ethics is the counsellor's own ethical and value system. But working as a counsellor may create a tension between personal ethics and the ethics that one considers appropriate to one's role. Bond (2000) uses an interesting example to illustrate this point. A counsellor learned that a friend was thinking about dating someone with a serious infectious illness. Would he be obliged to warn the friend? This would depend on how he had discovered that information. If he had discovered it from a social conversation he would feel that he had to warn the friend. However, if he had discovered the information through his work as a counsellor he would feel obliged to keep the information confidential. There is a distinction, therefore, between personal and professional ethics, and this is part of adapting to the professional role and taking into account the collective ethics of the profession.

Practitioners need to clearly understand their own values, and how these values may influence their work with clients. Tjeltveit (1986) has suggested a range of strategies for lessening the possibility of counsellors behaving in ways that are insensitive to clients' values:

- Become informed about the variety of values held in society
- Be aware of your own values
- Present value options to clients in an unbiased manner
- Be committed to clients' freedom of choice
- Respect clients with values that differ from your own
- Consult with others when necessary
- Consider referring clients to another counselor when substantial moral, religious, or political value differences exist. (Tjeltveit, 1986: 515–37)

However, simply relying on a combination of personal and professional ethics is sometimes not sufficient in resolving ethical dilemmas.

Bond (2000) illustrates this point with an example from a case:

Connie is seven months pregnant and has deeply held beliefs in favour of natural childbirth and against medical intervention. These feelings are being expressed by a refusal to accept a Caesarean delivery in order to protect both the foetus and herself from the consequences of dangerously high blood pressure. She has no illusions about the seriousness of her situation after nearly dying from similar complications in an earlier pregnancy. She has sought counselling to help her resist increasingly insistent offers of medical help. (Bond, 2000: 52)

Ethics and values within models of intervention

Bond (2000) points out that the practitioner's choice of approach has ethical implications and he shows how different therapeutic orientations incorporate different ethics and beliefs either implicitly or explicitly. Approaches to career counselling also vary in this way. In person-centred and developmental career counselling, for example, clients are assumed to have innate capacities for development, and they tend to be viewed as experts on how to achieve this. Ethics involving self-determination are therefore at the heart of these approaches. In contrast, the person–environment fit approach assumes that practitioners have some expert knowledge, and they will often take responsibility for administering tools that they see as in the client's best interests. Career counsellors with this orientation could be seen, therefore, as working within an ethic of welfare.

Agency policy

Counsellors working within an agency are usually required to follow specific procedures and protocols in relation to some ethical and therapeutic issues. Many counselling agencies, for example, have a policy that child protection takes precedence over individual client confidentiality.

Moral philosophy

Moral philosophy uses logical reasoning to consider ethical dilemmas. Professional ethics is a subsidiary area of moral philosophy which has as its main focus the core values that constitute professional identity. Perhaps the most highly developed form of professional ethics is the area of medical ethics. Bond (2000) points out that there is a wide range of approaches to medical ethics, and some writers argue that one particular philosophical model is both universally applicable and also superior to all the others. Other writers, however, have taken a less dogmatic approach, drawing on aspects of different models as appropriate. The most influential writers in this vein are Beauchamp and Childress

(1994), and their book, *Principles of Biomedical Ethics*, has had an important influence on the development of ethical principles for counselling and psychotherapy.

Beauchamp and Childress (1994) set out four major ethical principles:

- Respect for individual autonomy
- Beneficence (a commitment to benefiting the client)
- Non-maleficence (avoiding harm to the client)
- Justice (a fair distribution of services within society)

Others, for example, Kitchener (1984) have included fidelity (honouring the trust between client and counsellor).

As Bond (2000) argues, this combination of ethical principles as a basis for professional ethics has several advantages. The principles act as a 'metaphorical bridgehead' between the disciplines of moral philosophy and counselling. He also suggests that they provide counsellors with a greater level of ethical sophistication than they would be likely to gain from just reflecting on ethical dilemmas of their role from a practical point of view.

Some professional bodies in the field of counselling have included these principles within their ethical standards and codes. Examples include the American Counseling Association and the New Zealand Association of Counselors. However, as Bond (2000) notes, the principles do not transfer readily to some other cultures. As suggested earlier in this chapter, for example, individual autonomy is less important in some cultures than responsibility to the family. This suggests that this approach may have to be revised as counselling becomes a global activity.

Law

Practitioners need to have a basic familiarity with the law concerning contract, confidentiality, negligence, defamation, the protection and disclosure of records and acting as a witness. Bond (2000) has set out some basic principles for counsellors to follow in developing a basic understanding of the law. These can be summarised as follows:

- Refer to the most up-to-date law.
- Make a distinction between legislation and case law, as the former overrides the latter.
- Make sure you understand the legal basis for public or agency policy, especially if this affects the relationship between service users and service providers.
- Be aware that what is lawful for one public organisation may not apply to others or to independent or voluntary organisations.
- Consult a lawyer on important issues.

Professional codes and guidelines

Professional codes and guidelines will be the first point of reference for most practitioners. Breaching the terms of the code to which one is bound is a serious matter and can lead to formal complaints and disciplinary procedures being brought to play. However, Bond (2000) argues that the level of obligation is seldom such as to justify blind compliance. This would undermine the ethical basis of the counselling relationship, because it gives precedence to the code, over and above the relationship. He suggests that sometimes the more ethical response is to breach the code for carefully considered reasons. The ethical basis for breaching the code is strengthened if the practitioner is prepared to enter into a dialogue with the professional body, in order that the ethical basis for the decision can be examined, and, if appropriate, the code can be revised.

There is a fair amount of similarity in coverage across the codes of practice which different professional associations in therapeutic and career counselling have set out. Those most relevant to career counselling are the ethical standards of the (British) Institute for Career Guidance, the US National Career Development Association, the International Association for Educational and Vocational Guidance, and the British Association for Counselling and Psychotherapy. These can be obtained from these organisations' websites.

Most British and US codes of practice cover the issues of:

- Client safety
- Counsellor competence
- Respect for the client's self-determination
- Contracting
- Confidentiality
- Supervision
- Knowledge of relevant law
- Conduct of research
- Duty to maintain the profession's reputation

Practical guidelines on best practice for organisations delivering information, advice and guidance on learning and work have recently been developed in the UK by the Guidance Council. The 'Matrix standard' concerns only the delivery and management of services, and it consists of eight elements.

Those focusing on delivery are:

1 People are made aware of the service and how to engage with it.
2 People's use of the service is defined and understood.
3 People are provided with access to information and support in using it.
4 People are supported in exploring options and making choices.

Those concerned with managing the service are:

1 Service delivery is planned and maintained.
2 Staff competence and the support they are given are sufficient to deliver the service.
3 Feedback on the quality of the service is obtained.
4 Continuous quality improvement is ensured through monitoring, evaluation and action.

No reference is made in these standards, however, to the need for practitioners to adhere to any code of practice regarding the process of career support.

Niles and Harris-Bowlsbey (2002) suggest that some career counselling codes of practice seem to be inadequate in providing guidance to practitioners. First, in relation to the definition of a career counselling relationship, not all career interventions can be viewed as career counselling. Some, for instance, provide straightforward information. Secondly, ethical standards are lacking for the role of those who provide career support but are not professionally trained counsellors. This second point rather begs the question of what constitutes professional training in the UK. As we noted in the Introduction, those providing career support have very diverse backgrounds, both in training and in prior work experience, and there is very little agreement as to what professional training should involve.

Supervision

Most professional counselling and career counselling associations have some requirements concerning the supervision that their members should receive. For example, the statement of ethical standards provided by the International Association for Educational and Vocational Guidance includes the requirement that members 'seek and participate in regular supervision by which to increase the knowledge and skills required to effectively discharge their professional responsibilities and to develop goals for continued learning' (www.iaevg.org: 5). The American National Career Development Association, however, only requires that career counsellors have the '*Ability* to recognize own limitations as a career counselor and to seek supervision or refer clients *when appropriate*', and the '*Ability* to utilize supervision on a regular basis to maintain and improve counselor skills' (my italics). Mandatory supervision is not therefore a universal requirement. Also, many career practitioners in the UK are not members of any professional body and so will not have to adhere to any external ethical standards in this respect.

Nevertheless, many writers in this area agree that supervision is an important part of training and continuous professional development.

Discussing supervision in therapeutic counselling, McLeod (2003) identifies several different formats for the provision of supervision: individual sessions with the same person over a period of time; using separate supervisors to explore different issues; group supervision, with or without a designated leader; and supervision networks, where sets of colleagues make themselves available for mutual supervision.

The most common formats involve practitioners describing their work with a client to an individual supervisor, or to a group. As McLeod points out, however, this approach has several limitations. Practitioners appear to be selective in the material present, and may not discuss issues that may reflect badly on their competence. Also, fairly often, practitioners say that their supervision has been counterproductive. In the field of therapeutic counselling, debates have recently taken place about the appropriateness of adopting a mandatory system of supervision. Feltham (2000), for example, has expressed concern that a requirement for regular supervision may mean that the counselling profession becomes only open to those who are relatively affluent. And McLeod argues that a mandatory system of supervision could simply become a bureaucratic ritual, and as such could generate resistance.

There is little research evidence relating to the benefits of supervision. The only study known to this author of the supervision experiences of career counsellors is that of McMahon (2003), carried out in Australia. McMahon found that fewer than half the career counsellors surveyed received supervision. Those who did receive supervision found it helpful, however, and the greatest benefits were support, new ideas and strategies, feedback, debriefing and personal growth. The extent to which supervision made any difference to practice or to client outcomes was beyond the scope of the study, however.

Given the diverse range of contexts in which career practitioners work, and the wide variations in client needs, making supervision mandatory is likely to be problematic. Practitioners working in roles where they deal primarily with relatively straightforward requests for advice and information may not need regular supervision. It may be enough to simply encourage regular reflection on practice and continuous professional development. In contrast, career counsellors who spend most of their time working in-depth with clients who have more complex needs are likely to benefit from more formal supervisory relationships.

Summary

Several ethical issues that arise in the practice of career counselling were explored in the first part of this chapter: dual relationships; confidentiality; and accountability. In the second part, various sources of ethics were discussed: personal ethics; those implicit in therapeutic models; agency policy; moral philosophy; law; and professional codes of practice. Career counsellors need to find ways to reflect on ethical matters.

Supervision, as a component of continuing professional development, can provide the opportunity for discussion of ethical and moral issues as well as facilitating the development of other career counselling skills. Formal supervision may not be necessary in all contexts, however.

Discuss and Debate

1 Imagine a situation where your values could be in conflict with those of a client. How would you deal with this?
2 If you offer career support, what implicit and explicit values and ethical beliefs lie behind your preferred theoretical orientation? Are these values and ethics appropriate for all your clients?
3 What kinds of issues would be included in a statement of ethical standards for those who provide career support but have not been professionally trained in career counselling skills?

References

Ackerman, P.L. & Heggestad, E.D. (1997). Intelligence, personality and interests: evidence for overlapping traits. *Psychological Bulletin, 121,* 219–45.

Adams, J.D., Hayes, J. & Hopson, B. (1976). *Transition: understanding and managing personal change.* London: Martin Robertson.

Ali, L. & Graham, B. (1996). *The counselling approach to careers guidance.* London: Routledge.

Argyris, C. (1960). *Understanding organizational behavior.* Homewood, IL: Dorsey Press.

Arnold, J. (1997). *Managing careers into the 21st century.* London: Chapman.

Arnold, J. (2004). The congruence problem in John Holland's theory of vocational decisions. *Journal of Occupational and Organizational Psychology, 77,* 95–113.

Arthur, M.B. & Rousseau, D.M. (Eds.) (1996). *The boundaryless career.* New York: Oxford University Press.

Arthur, M.B., Claman, P.H. & DeFillipi, R.J. (1995). Intelligent enterprise, intelligent careers. *Academy of Management Executive, 9,* 7–22.

Arthur, M.B., Hall, D.T. & Lawrence, B.S. (1989). Generating new directions in career theory: the case for a transdisciplinary approach. In M.B. Arthur, D.T. Hall & B.S. Lawrence (Eds.), *Handbook of career theory.* Cambridge: Cambridge University Press.

Arthur, M.B., Inkson, K. & Pringle, J.K. (1999). *The new careers: individual action and economic change.* London: Sage.

Arthur, M.B., Khapova, S.N. & Wilderom, C.P.M. (2005). Career success in a boundaryless career world. *Journal of Organizational Behavior, 26,* 177–202.

Atchley, R.C. (1989). A continuity theory of normal aging. *The Gerontologist, 11,* 13–17.

Azrin, N.H., Flores, T. & Kaplan, S.J. (1975). Job-finding club: a group assisted program for obtaining employment. *Behavior Research and Therapy, 13,* 17–27.

Bailyn, L. (1989). Understanding individual experience at work: comments on the theory and practice of careers. In M.B. Arthur, D.T. Hall & B.S. Lawrence (Eds.), *Handbook of career theory.* Cambridge: Cambridge University Press.

Baker, M. & Kleijnen, J. (2000). The drive towards evidence-based health care. In N. Rowland & S. Goss (Eds.), *Evidence-based counselling and psychological therapies: research and applications.* London: Routledge.

Baltes, P.B. (1987). Theoretical propositions of life-span developmental psychology. *Developmental Psychology, 23,* 611–26.

Bandura, A. (1977). *Principles of behavior modification.* New York: Holt, Rinehart & Winston.

Bandura, A. (1986). *Social foundations of thought and action: a social cognitive theory.* Englewood Cliffs, NJ: Prentice Hall.

Bandura, A. (1997). *Self-efficacy: the exercise of control.* New York: Freeman.

Barrett-Lennard, G.T. (1986). The relationship inventory now: issues and advances in theory, method and use. In L.S. Greenberg & W.M. Pinsof (Eds.), *The psychotherapeutic process: a research handbook.* New York: Guilford.

Beauchamp, T.L. and Childress, J.F. (1974). *Principles of biomedical ethics.* Oxford: Oxford University Press.

Beck, A.T. (1976). *Cognitive therapy and the emotional disorders.* New York: International Universities Press.

Bedford, T. (1982). *Vocational guidance interviews: a survey by the Careers Service Inspectorate.* London: Careers Service Branch, Department of Employment.

Betz, N. (2004). Contributions of self-efficacy theory to career counseling: a personal perspective. *The Career Development Quarterly, 52,* 340–53.

Betz, N.E. & Luzzo, D. (1996). Career assessment and the Career Decision Making Self-Efficacy Scale. *Journal of Career Assessment, 4,* 313–28.

Betz, N.E., Harmon, L., & Borgen, F. (1996). The relationships of self-efficacy for the Holland themes to gender, occupational group membership, and vocational interests. *Journal of Counseling Psychology, 43,* 90–8.

Blocher, D.H. & Schutz, R.A. (1961). Relationships among self-descriptions, occupational stereotypes, and vocational preferences. *Journal of Counseling Psychology, 8,* 314–17.

Blustein, D.L. & Spengler, P.M. (1995). Personal adjustment: career counseling and psychotherapy. In W.B. Walsh & S.H. Osipow (Eds.), *Handbook of vocational psychology.* Mahwah, NJ: Erlbaum.

Bond, T. (2000). *Standards and ethics for counselling in action* (2nd ed.). London: Sage.

Bordin, E. (1979). The generalizability of the psychoanalytic concept of the working alliance. *Psychotherapy: Theory, Research and Practice, 16,* 252–60.

Bourdieu, P. & Passeron, J.C. (1977). *Reproduction in education, society and culture.* London: Sage.

Bowles, S. & Gintis, H. (1976). *Schooling in capitalist America.* London: Routledge.

Bozarth, J.D. & Fisher, R. (1990). Person-centered career counseling. In W.B. Walsh & S.H. Osipow (Eds.), *Handbook of vocational psychology.* Mahwah, NJ: Erlbaum.

Bozionelos, N. (2004). The relationship between disposition and career success: a British study. *Journal of Occupational and Organizational Psychology, 77,* 403–20.

Brown, D. (2002). The role of work values and cultural values in occupational choice, satisfaction, and success: a theoretical statement. In D. Brown & Associates, *Career choice and development* (4th ed.). San Francisco, CA: Jossey-Bass.

Brown, P. (1995). Cultural capital and social exclusion: some observations on recent trends in education, employment and the labour market. *Work, Employment and Society, 9,* 29–51.

Brown, S.D., Ryan Krane, N.E., Brecheisen, J., Castelino, P., Budism, I., Miller, M. & Edens, L. (2002). Critical ingredients of career choice interventions: more analyses and new hypotheses. *Journal of Vocational Behavior, 62,* 411–28.

Bruner, J. (2002). *Making stories: law, literature, life.* New York: Farrar, Strauss & Giroux.

Burchill, B.J., Day, D., Hudson, M., Ladipo, D., Mankelow, R., Nolan, J.P., Reed, H., Wichert, I.C. & Wilkinson, F. (1999). *Job insecurity and work intensification.* York: Joseph Rowntree Foundation.

Cattell, R.B., Eber, H.W. & Tatsuoka, M.M. (1970). *The 16–Factor Personality Questionnaire.* Champaign, IL: IPAT.

Chartrand, J.M. & Walsh, W.B. (2001). Career assessment: changes and trends. In F.T.L. Leong & A. Barak (Eds.), *Contemporary models in vocational psychology.* Mahwah, NJ: Erlbaum.

Chartered Institute for Personnel and Development (2003). *Managing employee careers: issues, trends and prospects.* London: CIPD.

Clark, A.E. & Oswald, A.J. (1996). Satisfaction and comparison income. *Journal of Public Economics, 61,* 359–81.

Cochran, L. (1997). *Career counseling: a narrative approach*. Thousand Oaks, CA: Sage.

Collin, A. (1996). Rethinking the relationship between theory and practice: practitioners as map-readers, map-makers – or jazz players? *British Journal of Guidance and Counselling, 24*, 67–81.

Conway, N. & Briner, R.B. (2002). Full-time versus part-time employees: understanding the links between work status, the psychological contract, and attitudes. *Journal of Vocational Behavior, 61*, 279–301.

Costa, P.T. & McCrae, R.R. (1992). *Revised NEO Personality Inventory (NEO PI-R) and NEO Five-Factor Inventory (NEO-FFI) professional manual*. Odessa, FL: Psychological Assessment Resources.

Crites, J.O. (1978). *Career Maturity Inventory*. Monterey, CA: California Test Bureau.

Davies, B. & Harre, R. (1990). Positioning and personhood. In R. Harre & L. van Langenhove (Eds.), *Positioning theory* (pp. 32–52). Oxford: Blackwell.

Dawis, R.V. & Lofquist, L.H. (1984). *A psychological theory of work adjustment: an individual difference model and its applications*. Minneapolis: University of Minnesota Press.

Doogan, K. (2001). Insecurity and long-term employment. *Work, Employment and Society, 15*, 419–41.

Dryden, W. (1979). Rational-emotive therapy and its contribution to careers counselling. *British Journal of Guidance and Counselling, 7*, 181–7.

Egan, G. (2002). *The skilled helper: a problem-management and opportunity-development approach to helping* (7th ed.). Pacific Grove, CA: Brooks/Cole.

Elliot, R., Shapiro, D., Firth-Cozens, J., Stiles, W.B., Hardy, G.E., Llewelyn, S.P. & Margison, F. (2001). Comprehensive process analysis of insight events in cognitive-behavioral and psychodynamic-interpersonal psychotherapies. In C.E. Hill (Ed.), *Helping skills: the empirical foundation*. Washington: APA.

Ellis, A. (1994). *Reason and emotion in psychotherapy*. New York: Birch Lane Press.

Erikson, E.H. (1959). Identity and the life-cycle. *Psychological Issues, 1*, 1–171.

Eysenck, H.J. (1972). The experimental study of Freudian concepts. *Bulletin of the British Psychological Society, 25*, 261–7.

Feltham, C. (2000). Counselling supervision: baselines, problems and possibilities. In B. Lawton & C. Feltham (Eds.), *Taking supervision forward: enquiries and trends in counselling and psychotherapy*. London: Sage.

Fitzgerald, L. & Harmon, L. (2001). Women's career development: a postmodern update. In F.T.L. Leong & A. Barak (Eds.), *Contemporary models in vocational psychology*. Mahwah: Erlbaum.

Fouad, N.A. & Smith, P.L. (1996). Test of a social cognitive model for middle school students: math and science. *Journal of Counseling Psychology, 43*, 338–46.

Fretz, B.R. (2001). Postural movements in a counseling dyad. In C.E. Hill (Ed.), *Helping skills: the empirical foundation*. Washington: APA.

Freud, S. (1933/1973). *New introductory lectures on psycho-analysis*. Harmondsworth: Penguin.

Gallos, J.V. (1989). Exploring women's development: implications for career theory, practice and research. In M.B. Arthur, D.T. Hall & B.S. Lawrence (Eds.), *Handbook of career theory*. Cambridge: Cambridge University Press.

Giddens, A. (1984). *The constitution of society*. Cambridge: Polity Press.

Gilligan, C. (1982). *In a different voice: psychological theory and women's development*. Cambridge, MA: Harvard University Press.

Gonclaves, O.F. (1995). Hermeneutics, constructivism and cognitive-behavioral therapies: from the object to the project. In R.A. Neimeyer & M.J. Mahoney

(Eds.), *Constructivism in psychotherapy.* Washington, DC: American Psychological Association.

Gould, R.L. (1978). *Transformations: growth and change in adult life.* New York: Simon & Schuster.

Grant, A.M. & Greene, J. (2001). *Coach yourself: make real change in your life.* London: Momentum Press.

Gysbers, N.C., Heppner, M.J. & Johnston, J.A. (2003). *Career counseling: process, issues, and techniques* (2nd ed.). Boston: Allyn and Bacon.

Hackett, G. & Betz, N.E. (1981). A self-efficacy approach to the career development of women. *Journal of Vocational Behavior, 18,* 326–39.

Hall, D.T. (2002). *Careers in and out of organizations.* Thousand Oaks, CA: Sage.

Hall, D.T. & Chandler, D.E. (2005). Psychological success: when the career is a calling. *Journal of Organizational Behavior, 26,* 155–76.

Hall, D.T. & Mirvis, P.H. (1996). The new protean career: psychological success and the path with a heart. In D.T. Hall & Associates, *The career is dead – long live the career: a relational approach to careers.* San Francisco: Jossey Bass.

Hanson, W.E., Claiborn, C.D. & Kerr, B. (1997). Differential effects of two test-interpretation styles in counseling: a field study. *Journal of Counseling Psychology, 44,* 400–5.

Harmon, L.W., Hansen, J.C., Borgen, F.H. & Hammer, A.L. (1994). *Strong Interest Inventory: applications and technical guide.* Palo Alto, CA: Consulting Psychologists Press.

Hawthorn, R., Killeen, J., Kidd, J.M. & Watts, A.G. (2003). *Career planning and career guidance: mapping the research base.* Cambridge: NICEC.

Herr, E.L. (1997). Career counseling: a process in process. *British Journal of Guidance & Counselling, 25,* 81–93.

Herriot, P. & Pemberton, C. (1996). Contracting careers. *Human Relations, 49,* 757–90.

Hesketh, B. (2000). The next millennium of 'fit' research: comments on 'The congruence myth: an analysis of the efficacy of the person-environment fit model' by H.E.A. Tinsley. *Journal of Vocational Behavior, 56,* 190–6.

Hill, C.E. (2001). Introduction. In C.E. Hill (Ed.), *Helping skills: the empirical foundation.* Washington: APA.

Hill, C.E., Helms, J.E., Tichenor, V., Spiegel, S.B., O'Grady, K.E. & Perry, E.S. (2001). Effects of therapist response modes in brief psychotherapy. In C.E. Hill (Ed.), *Helping skills: the empirical foundation.* Washington: APA.

Hirsh, W. & Jackson, C. (1994). *Successful career planning in a week.* London: Hodder & Stoughton.

Hirsh, W., Kidd, J.M. & Watts, A.G. (1998). *Constructs of work used in career guidance.* Cambridge: National Institute for Careers Education and Counselling.

Hofstede, G. (2001). *Culture's consequences: comparing values, behaviors, institutions, and organizations across nations.* Thousand Oaks, CA: Sage.

Hogan, D.P. (1980). The transition to adulthood as a career contingency. *American Sociological Review, 45,* 573–86.

Holland, J.L. (1985a). *Making vocational choices: a theory of vocational personalities and work environments.* Englewood Cliffs, NJ: Prentice-Hall.

Holland, J.L. (1985b). *Manual for the Vocational Preference Inventory.* Odessa, FL: Psychological Assessment Resources.

Holland, J.L. (1985c). *The self-directed search: professional manual.* Odessa, FL: Psychological Assessment Resources.

Holland, J.L. (1997). *Making vocational choices* (3rd ed.). Odessa, FL: Psychological Assessment Resources.

Holland, J.L., Magoon, T.M. & Spokane, A.R. (1981). Counseling psychology: career interventions, research, and theory. *Annual Review of Psychology, 32,* 279–305.

Holmes, J. & Lindley, R. (1991). *The values of psychotherapy.* Oxford: Oxford University Press.

Humphries, M. & Dyer, S. (2005). Women, work and career development: equal employment opportunity or employment equity? In B. Irving & B. Malik (Eds.), *Critical reflections on career education and guidance: promoting social justice within a global economy.* Abingdon: RoutledgeFalmer.

Hunt, E.P. & Smith, P. (1944). *Scientific vocational guidance and its value to the choice of employment work of a local education authority.* Birmingham: City of Birmingham Education Committee.

Irving, B.A. (2005). Social justice: a context for career education and guidance. In B. Irving & B. Malik (Eds.), *Critical reflections on career education and guidance: promoting social justice within a global economy.* Abingdon: RoutledgeFalmer.

Ivey, A.E. & Authior, J. (1978). *Microcounseling: innovations in interviewing, counseling, psychotherapy and psychoeducation* (2nd ed.). Springfield, IL: Charles C. Thomas.

Jackson, C. (1996). *Understanding psychological testing.* Leicester: BPS Books.

Jacobs, M. (1999). *Psychodynamic counselling in action.* London: Sage.

Jacobs, S. (1999). Trends in women's career patterns and in gender occupational mobility in Britain. *Gender, Work & Organization, 6,* 32–46.

Jepsen, D.A. (1996). Relationships between developmental career counseling theory and practice. In M.L. Savickas & W.B. Walsh (Eds.), *Handbook of career counseling theory and practice.* Palo Alto, CA: Davies-Black.

Jepsen, D.A. & Sheu, H.B. (2003). General job satisfaction from a developmental perspective: exploring choice-job matches at two career stages. *The Career Development Quarterly, 52,* 162–79.

Kahn, W.A. (1996). Secure base relationships at work. In D.T. Hall (Ed.), *The career is dead – long live the career.* San Francisco: Jossey-Bass.

Kanter, R.M. (1977). *Men and women of the corporation.* New York: Basic Books.

Katz, M.R. (1969). Can computers make guidance decisions for students? *College Board Review, 72.*

Keele, R. (1986). Mentoring or networking? Strong and weak ties in career development. In L. Moore (Ed.), *Not as far as you think: the realities of working women.* Lexington, MA: Lexington.

Kelly, G.A. (1955). *The psychology of personal constructs, volumes 1 and 2.* New York: W.W. Norton.

Kidd, J.M. (1981). The assessment of career development. In A.G. Watts, D.E. Super & J.M. Kidd (Eds.), *Career development in Britain.* Cambridge: CRAC.

Kidd, J.M. (1984a). The relationship of self and occupational concepts to the occupational preferences of adolescents. *Journal of Vocational Behavior, 24,* 48–65.

Kidd, J.M. (1984b). Young people's perceptions of their occupational decision making. *British Journal of Guidance & Counselling, 12,* 25–38.

Kidd, J.M. (1988). *Assessment in action.* Leicester: NIACE.

Kidd, J.M. (1996). The career counselling interview. In A.G. Watts, B. Law, J. Killeen, J.M. Kidd & R. Hawthorn, *Rethinking careers education and guidance: theory, policy and practice.* London: Routledge.

Kidd, J.M. (1998). Emotion: an absent presence in career theory. *Journal of Vocational Behavior, 52,* 275–88.

Kidd, J.M. (2003). Career development work with individuals, In R. Woolfe, W. Dryden & S. Strawbridge (Eds.), *Handbook of Counselling Psychology.* London: Sage.

Kidd, J.M. (2004). Emotion in career contexts: challenges for theory and research. *Journal of Vocational Behavior, 64,* 441–54.

Kidd, J.M. & Killeen, J. (1992). Are the effects of careers guidance worth having? Changes in practice and outcomes. *Journal of Occupational and Organizational Psychology, 65,* 219–34.

Kidd, J.M., Hirsh, W. & Jackson, C. (2004). Straight talking: the nature of effective career discussion at work. *Journal of Career Development, 30,* 231–45.

Kidd, J.M., Killeen, J., Jarvis, J. & Offer, M. (1993). *Working models of career guidance: the interview.* Report to the Employment Department. Birkbeck College, University of London.

Kidd, J.M., Killeen, J., Jarvis, J. & Offer, M. (1997). Competing schools or stylistic variation in careers guidance interviewing. *British Journal of Guidance & Counselling, 25,* 47–65.

Killeen, J. (1996). The learning and economic outcomes of guidance. In A.G.Watts, B. Law, J. Killeen, J.M. Kidd & R. Hawthorn, *Rethinking careers education and guidance: theory, policy and practice.* London: Routledge.

Killeen, J. & White, M. (2000). *The impact of career guidance on adult employed people.* Research Report RR226. Sheffield: Department for Education and Employment.

Killeen, J., Kidd, J.M., Watts, A.G. & Hawthorn, R. (2003). *Career planning and career guidance: mapping the research base.* Annexes and Bibliography. Cambridge: NICEC.

Kitchener, K.S. (1984). Intuition, critical evaluation and ethical principles: the foundation for ethical decisions in counseling psychology. *Counseling Psychologist, 12,* 43–55.

Knox, S., Hess, S.A., Petersen, D.A. & Hill, C.E. (2001). A qualitative analysis of client perceptions of the effects of helpful therapist self-disclosure in long-term therapy. In C.E. Hill (Ed.), *Helping skills: the empirical foundation.* Washington: APA.

Kolb, D.A. (1976). *Experiential learning.* Englewood Cliffs, NJ: Prentice-Hall.

Krett, K. (1985). Maternity, paternity, and child-care policies. *Personnel Administration, 30,* 125–36.

Krumboltz, J.D. (1988). *Career Beliefs Inventory.* Palo Alto, CA: Consulting Psychologists Press.

Law, B. (1981). Careers theory: a third dimension? In A.G. Watts, D.E. Super & J.M. Kidd (Eds.), *Career development in Britain.* Cambridge: CRAC.

Law, B. (1996). A career-learning theory. In A.G. Watts, B. Law, J. Killeen, J.M. Kidd & R. Hawthorn, *Rethinking careers education and guidance: theory, policy and practice.* London: Routledge.

Law, B. & Ward, R. (1981). Is career development motivated? In A.G. Watts, D.E. Super & J.M. Kidd (Eds.), *Career development in Britain.* Cambridge: CRAC.

Law, B. & Watts, A.G. (1977). *Schools, careers and community.* London: Church Information Office.

Law, B., Meijers, F. & Wijers, G. (2002). New perspectives on career and identity in the contemporary world. *British Journal of Guidance & Counselling, 30,* 431–49.

Lawrence, B.S. (1980). The myth of the midlife crisis. *Sloan Management Review, 21,* 35–49.

Lawrence, B.S. (1984). Age grading: the implicit organizational timetable. *Journal of Occupational Behavior, 5,* 23–35.

Lehman, D.R., Chiu, C. & Schaller, M. (2004). Psychology and culture. *Annual Review of Psychology, 55,* 689–714.

Lent, E.B. (1996). The person focus in career theory and practice. In M.L. Savickas & W.B. Walsh (Eds.), *Handbook of career counseling theory and practice.* Palo Alto, CA: Davies-Black.

Lent, R.W., Brown, S.D. & Hackett, G. (1994). Toward a unifying social cognitive theory of career and academic interest, choice, and performance. *Journal of Vocational Behavior, 45,* 79–122.

Leong, F.T.L. & Hartung, P.J. (2000). Adapting to the changing multicultural context of career. In A. Collin & R. Young (Eds.), *The future of career.* Cambridge: Cambridge University Press.

Levinson, D.J., Darrow, D.C., Klein, E.B., Levinson, M.H. & McKee, B. (1978). *The seasons of a man's life.* New York: Knopf.

Levinson, D.J. & Levinson, J.D. (1996). *The seasons of a woman's life.* New York: Knopf.

Lincoln, Y.S. & Guba, E.G. (2000). Paradigmatic controversies, contradictions and emerging confluences. In N.K. Denzin & Y.S. Lincoln (Eds.), *Handbook of qualitative research* (2nd ed.). Thousand Oaks, CA: Sage.

Lock, A., Epston, D., Maisel, R. & de Faria, N. (2005). Resisting anorexia/bulimia: Foucauldian perspectives in narrative therapy. *British Journal of Guidance & Counselling, 33,* 315–32.

London, M. (1983). Toward a theory of career motivation. *Academy of Management Review, 8,* 620–30.

Luborksy, L. and Crits-Christoph, P. (Eds.) (1990). *Understanding transference: the CCRT method.* New York: Basic Books.

Luborsky, L., Popp, C., Luborsky, E. & Mark, D. (1994). The core conflictual relationship theme. *Psychotherapy Research, 4,* 172–83.

March, J. & Simon, H. (1958). *Organizations.* New York: Wiley.

Matthews, G. & Deary, I.J. (1998). *Personality traits.* Cambridge: Cambridge University Press.

McAdams, D.P. (1997). *Stories we live by. Personal myths and the making of the self.* New York: Guilford Press.

McLeod, J. (2001). *Qualitative research in counselling and psychotherapy.* London: Sage.

McLeod, J. (2003). *Introduction to counselling.* Buckingham: Open University Press.

McMahon, M. (2003). Supervision and career counsellors: a little-explored practice with an uncertain future. *British Journal of Guidance & Counselling, 31,* 177–87.

McOrmond, T. (2004). Changes in working trends over the past decade. *Labour Market Trends,* January, 25–35.

Mead, G.H. (1934). *Mind, self and society.* Chicago: University of Chicago Press.

Mignot, P. (2001). Working with individuals. In B. Gothard, P. Mignot, M. Offer & M. Ruff, *Careers guidance in context.* London: Sage.

Miller, R., Crute, V. & Hargie, O. (1992). *Professional interviewing.* London: Routledge.

Mitchell, L.K. & Krumboltz, J.D. (1996). Social learning approach to career decision making: Krumboltz's theory. In D. Brown, L. Brooks & Associates (Eds.), *Career choice and development: applying contemporary theories to practice* (3rd ed.). San Francisco, CA: Jossey-Bass.

Multon, K.D., Ellis-Kalton, C.A., Heppner, M.J. & Gysbers, N.C. (2003). The relationship between counselor verbal response modes and the working alliance in career counselling. *The Career Development Quarterly, 51,* 259–73.

Myers, I.B. & McCaulley, M. (1985). *Manual: a guide to the use of the Myers-Briggs Type Indicator.* New York: Consulting Psychologists Press.

Nathan, R. & Hill, L. (2006). *Career counselling* (2nd ed.). London: Sage.

Nicholson, J. (1980). *Seven ages.* London: Collins.

Nicholson, N. (1990). The transition cycle: causes, outcomes, processes and forms. In S. Fischer & C.L. Cooper (Eds.), *On the move: the psychology of change and transition.* Chichester: Wiley.

Nicholson, N. & West, M. (1988). *Managerial job change: men and women in transition.* Cambridge: Cambridge University Press.

Nicholson, N. & de Waal-Andrews, W. (2005). Playing to win: biological imperatives, self-regulation, and trade-offs in the game of career success. *Journal of Organizational Behavior, 26,* 137–54.

Niles, S.G. & Harris-Bowlsbey, J. (2002). *Career development interventions in the 21st century.* New Jersey: Merrill Prentice-Hall.

Norcross, J.C. & Grencavage, L.M. (1989). Eclecticism and integration in counselling and psychotherapy: major themes and obstacles. *British Journal of Guidance and Counselling, 17,* 215–47.

Norcross, J.C. & Thomas, B.L. (1988). What's stopping us now? Obstacles to psychotherapy integration. *Journal of Integrative and Eclectic Psychotherapy, 7,* 74–80.

OECD (2003) *OECD review of career guidance policies: United Kingdom country note.* Paris: OECD.

Offer, M. (1997). *Supporting careers guidance in an information society.* Dublin: National Centre for Guidance in Education.

Offer, M. (2000). *Careers professionals' guide to the internet.* Richmond: Trotman.

Offer, M. (2001). The discourse of the labour market. In B. Gothard, P. Mignot, M. Offer & M. Ruff, *Careers guidance in context.* London: Sage.

Oliver, L.W. & Zack, J.S. (1999). Career assessment on the internet: an exploratory study. *Journal of Career Assessment, 7,* 323–56.

Ornstein, S. & Isabella, L. (1990). Age vs. stage models of career attitudes of women: a partial replication and extension. *Journal of Vocational Behavior, 36,* 1–19.

Osipow, S.H., Carney, C.G., Winer, J.L., Yanico, B. & Koschier, M. (1997). *The Career Decision Scale.* Odessa, FL: Psychological Assessment Resources.

Owen, I.R. (1999). Exploring the similarities and differences between person-centred and psychodynamic therapy. *British Journal of Guidance and Counselling, 27,* 165–78.

Parker, P. (2002). Working with the Intelligent Career Model. *Journal of Employment Counseling, 39,* 83–96.

Parsons, F. (1909). *Choosing a vocation.* Boston: Houghton Mifflin.

Patterson, P. (1964). Counseling: self-clarification and the helping relationship. In H. Borow (Ed.), *Man in a world of work.* Boston: Houghton Mifflin.

Phillips, S.D., Christopher-Sisk, E.K. & Gravino, K.L. (2001). Making career decisions in a relational context. *The Counseling Psychologist, 29,* 193–213.

Pogson, C.E., Cober, A.B., Doverspike, D. & Rogers, J.R. (2003). Differences in self-reported work ethic across three career stages. *Journal of Vocational Behavior, 62,* 189–201.

Ponterotto, J.G. & Grieger, I. (1999). Merging qualitative and quantitative perspectives in a research identity. In M. Kopala & L. Suzuki (Eds.), *Using qualitative methods in psychology.* Thousand Oaks, CA: Sage.

Pope, K.S. (1991). Dual relationships in psychotherapy. *Ethics and Behavior, 1,* 21–34.

Powell, G.N. & Mainiero, L.A. (1992). Cross-currents in the river of time: conceptualizing the complexities of women's careers. *Journal of Management, 18,* 215–37.

Prediger, D.J. (2000). Holland's hexagon is alive and well – though somewhat out of shape: response to Tinsley. *Journal of Vocational Behavior, 56,* 197–204.

Premack, S.L. & Wanous, J.P. (1985). A meta-analysis of realistic job preview experiments. *Journal of Applied Psychology, 70,* 706–19.

Prince, J.P., Most, R.B. & Silver, D.G. (2003). Self-help career assessment: ethical and professional issues. *Journal of Career Assessment, 11,* 40–58.

Ridley, C.R. & Lingle, D.W. (1996). Cultural empathy in multicultural counseling: a multidimensional process model. In P.B. Pedersen, J.G. Draguns, W.J. Lonner & J.E. Trimble (Eds.), *Counseling across cultures*. London: Sage.

Roberts, K. (1968). The entry into employment: an approach towards a general theory. *Sociological Review, 16,* 165–84.

Roberts, K. (1997). Prolonged transitions to uncertain destinations: the implications for careers guidance. *British Journal of Guidance & Counselling, 25,* 345–60.

Roberts, K. (2005). Social class, opportunity structures and career guidance. In B.A. Irving & B. Malik (Eds.), *Critical reflections on career education and guidance: promoting social justice within a global economy*. Abingdon: RoutledgeFalmer.

Rodger, A. (1952). *The Seven-Point plan*. London: NIIP.

Rogers, C.R. (1942). *Counseling and psychotherapy*. Boston: Houghton Mifflin.

Rogers, C.R. (1957). The necessary and sufficient conditions of therapeutic personality change. *Journal of Consulting Psychology, 21,* 95–103.

Rogers, C.R. (1986). Client-centered therapy. In I.L. Kutush & A.Wolf (Eds.), *Psychotherapists' casebook: theory and technique in the practice of modern therapies*. San Francisco: Jossey-Bass.

Rounds, J.B. & Tracey, T.J. (1990). From trait-and-factor to person-environment fit counseling: theory and process. In W.B. Walsh & S.H. Osipow (Eds.), *Career counseling: contemporary topics in vocational psychology*. Hillsdale, NJ: Erlbaum.

Rounds, J.B., Henley, G.A., Dawis, R.V., Lofquist, L.H. & Weiss, D.J. (1981). *Manual for the Minnesota Importance Questionnaire*. Minneapolis, MN: Vocational Psychology Research, Department of Psychology, University of Minnesota.

Rousseau, D.M. (1990). New hire perceptions of their own and their employer's obligations: a study of psychological contracts. *Journal of Organizational Behavior, 11,* 389–400.

Salovey, P. & Mayer, J.D. (1990). Emotional intelligence. *Imagination, Cognition and Personality, 9,* 185–211.

Sampson, JP., Jr., Peterson, G.W., Reardon, R.C. & Lenz, J.G. (2000). *Designing career services to cost-effectively meet individual needs*. Tallahassee: Florida State University, Center for the Study of Technology in Counseling and Career Development.

Sapsford, R. (1984). Levels of analysis. In R. Stevens, *D307 social psychology: metablock*. Milton Keynes: Open University Press.

Savickas, M.L. (2005). The theory and practice of career construction. In S.D. Brown & R.W. Lent (Eds.), *Career development and counseling: putting theory and research to work*. Hoboken, NJ: John Wiley & Sons.

Saville, P., Holdsworth, R., Nyfield, G., Cramp, L. & Mabey, W. (1984). *Occupational Personality Questionnaire Manual*. Thames Ditton: Saville and Holdsworth Ltd.

Schein, E.H. (1993). *Career anchors: discovering your real values*. San Diego, CA: Pfeiffer.

Schlossberg, N.K. (1981). A model for analysing human adaptation to transition. *The Counseling Psychologist, 9,* 2–18.

Schlossberg, N.K., Troll, L.E. & Leibowitz, Z. (1978). *Perspectives on counseling adults: issues and skills*. Monterey: Brooks/Cole.

Schneider, B., Goldstein, H.W. & Smith, D.B. (1995). The ASA framework: an update. *Personnel Psychology, 48,* 747–73.

Schon, D. (1983). *The reflective practitioner: how professionals think in action*. London: Temple Smith.

Scott, M.J. & Dryden, W. (2003). The cognitive-behavioural paradigm. In R. Woolfe, W. Dryden & S. Strawbridge (Eds.), *Handbook of counselling psychology* (2nd ed.). London: Sage.

Sekaran, U. & Hall, D.T. (1989). Asynchronism in dual-career and family linkages. In M.B. Arthur, D.T. Hall & B.S. Lawrence (Eds.), *Handbook of career theory.* Cambridge: Cambridge University Press.

Sennett, R. (1998). *The corrosion of character: the personal consequences of work in the new capitalism.* New York: Norton.

Sheehy, G. (1976). *Passages: predictable crises of adult life.* New York: Datron.

Sherif, M. (1936). *The psychology of social norms.* New York: Harper & Row.

Simon, J. & Osipow, S.H. (1996). Continuity of career: the vocational script in counseling older workers. *The Career Development Quarterly, 45,* 152–62.

Sinclair, S.L. & Monk, G. (2005). Discursive empathy: a new foundation for therapeutic practice. *British Journal of Guidance & Counselling, 35,* 333–49.

Smith, M.L. & Glass, G.V. (1977). Meta-analysis of psychotherapy outcome studies. *American Psychologist, 32,* 752–60.

Spokane, A.R. (1985). A review of research on person-environment congruence in Holland's theory of careers. *Journal of Vocational Behavior, 31,* 37–44.

Spokane, A.R. (1991). *Career intervention.* Englewood Cliffs, NJ: Prentice-Hall.

Storey, J.A. (2000). 'Fracture lines' in the career environment. In A. Collin & R.A. Young (Eds.), *The future of career.* Cambridge: Cambridge University Press.

Strawson, G. (2004). Tales of the unexpected. A review of J. Bruner (2002), Making Stories: Law, Literature, Life. *The Guardian,* 10 January.

Strupp, H.H. (1973). On the basic ingredients of psychotherapy. *Journal of Clinical and Consulting Psychology, 41,* 1–8.

Sugarman, L. (1992). Ethical issues in counselling at work. *British Journal of Guidance & Counselling, 20,* 64–74.

Sugarman, L. (2001). *Life-span development: concepts, theories and interventions.* London: Methuen.

Super, D.E. (1957). *The psychology of careers.* New York: Harper & Row.

Super, D.E. (1963). Toward making self-concept theory operational. In D.E. Super, R. Starishevsky, N. Matlin & J.P. Jordaan (Eds.), *Career development: self-concept theory.* New York: College Entrance Examination Board.

Super, D.E. (1974). *Measuring vocational maturity for counseling and evaluation.* Washington, DC: American Personnel and Guidance Association.

Super, D.E. (1980). A life-span, life-space approach to career development. *Journal of Vocational Behavior, 16,* 282–98.

Super, D.E. & Overstreet, P.L. (1960). *The vocational maturity of ninth grade boys.* New York: Teachers College, Columbia University.

Super, D.E., Thompson, A.S., Lindeman, R.E., Jordaan, J.P. & Myers, R.A. (1981). *Career development inventory.* Palo Alto, CA: Consulting Psychologists Press.

Super, D.E., Thompson, A.S., Lindeman, R.H., Myers, R.A., & Jordaan, J.P. (1988). *Adult career concerns inventory.* Palo Alto, CA: Consulting Psychologists Press.

Swanson, J.L. (1996). The theory *is* the practice: trait-and-factor/person-environment fit counseling. In M.L. Savickas & W.B. Walsh (Eds.), *Handbook of career counseling theory and practice.* Palo Alto, CA: Davies-Black.

Swanson, J.L. & Fouad, N.A. (1999). *Career theory and practice.* Thousand Oaks, CA: Sage.

Taylor, N.B. (1985). How do career counsellors counsel? *British Journal of Guidance & Counselling, 13,* 166–77.

Taylor, R. (2003). *Britain's world of work – myths and realities.* Swindon: ESRC.

Tepper, D.T. & Haase, R.P. (2001). Verbal and nonverbal communication of facilitative conditions. In C.E. Hill (Ed.), *Helping skills: the empirical foundation.* Washington: APA.

Tinsley, H.E.A. (2000). The congruence myth: an analysis of the efficacy of the person-environment fit model. *Journal of Vocational Behavior, 56,* 147–79.

Tjeltveit, A.C. (1986). The ethics of value conversion in psychotherapy: appropriate and inappropriate therapist influence on client values. *Clinical Psychology Review, 6,* 515–37.

Toker, D.M., Fischer, A.R. & Subich, L.M. (1998). Personality and vocational behavior: a selective review of the literature. *Journal of Vocational Behavior, 53,* 115–53.

Tranberg, M., Slane, S. & Ekeberg, S.E. (1993). The relationship between interest congruence and satisfaction: a meta-analysis. *Journal of Vocational Behavior, 42,* 253–64.

Tyers, C. & Sinclair, A. (2005). *Intermediate impacts of advice and guidance.* Research Report RR638. London: DFES.

Vaillant, G.E. (1977). *Adaptation to life.* Boston: Little, Brown & Co.

Wampold, B.E. (2000). Outcomes of individual counseling and psychotherapy: empirical evidence addressing two fundamental questions. In S.D. Brown & R.W. Lent (Eds.), *Handbook of counseling psychology* (3rd ed.). New York: Wiley.

Warr, P.B. (2002). The study of well-being, behaviour and attitudes. In P.B. Warr (Ed.), *Psychology at work.* London: Penguin.

Watkins, C.E. & Savickas, M.L (1990) Psychodynamic career counseling. In W.B. Walsh & S.H. Osipow (Eds.), *Career counseling: contemporary topics in vocational psychology.* Hillsdale, NJ: Erlbaum.

Watson, J.B. (1919). *Psychology from the standpoint of a behaviorist.* Philadelphia: J.B. Lippincott.

Watson, G. & Glaser, E.M. (1994). *Watson-Glaser Critical Thinking Appraisal Manual.* San Antonio, TX: Psychological Corporation.

Watts, A.G. (1996a). Socio-political ideologies in guidance. In A.G.Watts, B. Law, J. Killeen, J.M. Kidd & R. Hawthorn, *Rethinking careers education and guidance: theory, policy and practice.* London: Routledge.

Watts, A.G. (1996b). Computers in guidance. In A.G.Watts, B. Law, J. Killeen, J.M. Kidd & R. Hawthorn, *Rethinking careers education and guidance: theory, policy and practice.* London: Routledge.

Watts, A.G. (1996c). Careers guidance and public policy. In A.G.Watts, B. Law, J. Killeen, J.M. Kidd & R. Hawthorn, *Rethinking careers education and guidance: theory, policy and practice.* London: Routledge.

Watts, A.G. (2001). Career guidance and social exclusion: a cautionary tale. *British Journal of Guidance & Counselling, 29,* 157–76.

Watts, A.G. & Kidd, J.M. (1978). Evaluating the effectiveness of careers guidance: a review of the British research. *Journal of Occupational Psychology, 51,* 235–48.

Watts, A.G. & Sadler, J. (2000). *Quality Guidance: a sectoral analysis.* Cambridge: CRAC/GAB.

Watts, A.G. & Sultana, R.G. (2004). *Career guidance policies in 37 countries: contrasts and common themes.* Thessaloniki: CEDEFOP.

Watts, A.G., Hughes, D. & Wood, M. (2005). *A market in career? Evidence and issues.* Derby: Centre for Guidance Studies, University of Derby.

Watts, A.G., Law, B. & Fawcett, B. (1981). Some implications for guidance practice. In A.G. Watts, D.E. Super & J.M. Kidd (Eds.), *Career development in Britain: some contributions to theory and practice.* Cambridge: CRAC.

Wetherington, E., Kessler, R.C. & Pixley, J.E. (2004). Turning points in adulthood. In O.G. Brim, C.D. Ryff, & R.C. Kessler, (Eds.), *How healthy are we? A national study of well-being at midlife.* Chicago: University of Chicago Press.

Whiston, S.C., Sexton, T.L. & Lasoff, D.L. (1998). Career-intervention outcome: a replication and extension of Oliver and Spokane (1988). *Journal of Counseling Psychology, 45,* 150–65.

Whiston, S.C., Brecheisen, T.L. & Stephens, J. (2003). Does treatment modality affect career counseling effectiveness? *Journal of Vocational Behavior, 62,* 390–410.

White, M. & Epston, D. (1990). *Narrative means to therapeutic ends.* New York: Norton.

Wilden, S. & La Gro, N. (1998). New frameworks for careers guidance: developing a conceptual model of the interview. *British Journal of Guidance & Counselling, 26,* 175–93.

Wilkins, P. (2000). Unconditional positive regard reconsidered. *British Journal of Guidance & Counselling, 28,* 23–37.

Winslade, J.M. (2005). Utilising discursive positioning in counselling. *British Journal of Guidance & Counselling, 35,* 351–64.

Index

This index is in word-by-word order. Figures in *italics* indicate diagrams.